Watercolor Quilts

That Patchwork Place®

Pat Maixner Magaret & Donna Ingram Slusser

Credits

Editor . . . . .Barbara Weiland
Copy Editor . . . . .Liz McGehee
Text and Cover Design . . . . .Joanne Lauterjung
Managing Editor . . . . .Greg Sharp
Typesetting . . . . .Joanne Lauterjung
Photography . . . . .Brent Kane
Illustration and Graphics . . . . .Laurel Strand
Stephanie Benson

Watercolor Quilts©
©1993 by Pat Maixner Magaret and Donna Slusser

That Patchwork Place®
is an imprint of Martingale & Company™
20205 144th Ave. NE, Woodinville, WA 98072-8478

Printed in Hong Kong
05 04 03   21 20 19 18

Library of Congress Cataloging-in-Publication Data
Magaret, Pat Maixner,
        Watercolor quilts / Pat Maixner Magaret & Donna Ingram
        Slusser.
            p.   cm.
        Includes bibliographical references.
        ISBN 1-56477-031-1 :
        1. Quilting.   2. Patchwork.   I. Slusser, Donna Ingram
    II. Title.
    TT835.M2715   1993
    746.3–dc20   93-8551
                                                                        CIP

DEDICATION

To our families:

Our parents, Frank and Betty Maixner, and Marvin and Lois Ingram, who gave us skills and taught us the value of working hard in order to accomplish our goals;

Our husbands, David Magaret and Lloyd Slusser, who inspire us to spread our wings and fly in new directions;

Our children, Craig, Nathan, and Anna Magaret; and Alan Martinson, Kirstin Martinson, and Larry Slusser, who not only sleep under our quilts but encourage us to continue making more.

ACKNOWLEDGMENTS

Our wholehearted thanks to:

Deirdre Amsden, who started the Colourwash concept and whose generous spirit has taken us beyond the boundaries of traditional quiltmaking;

Our students, who have been willing to work with design concepts rather than specific patterns—you have taught us more than you could ever know;

Our quilting friends—old and new: members of Patchin' People, Stitch 'n Study, and Palouse Patchers, and our new quilting friends, who remind us that quilts are a common and special bond wherever one travels;

The quiltmakers whose efforts are pictured in this book: Annie Bacon, Marilyn Bafus, Adele Bingham, Kerry Bloxham, Thine Bloxham, Kathleen Butts, Lisa Calhoun, Eleanor Cole, Judy Dobbelstein, Rosy Ferner, Margaret Fortune, Myrtle Fulfs, Karla Harris, Yumiko Hirasawa, Lucy Kittrick, Ellen Krieger, Tammy Lydeen, Judy Abdel-Monem, Anne Morton, Ree Nancarrow, Lisa Nicholson, Karen Pederson, Janie Perino, Shirley Perryman, Kathy Pole, Nancy Larson-Powers, Jeanie Renfro, J. J. Scheri, Daleah Thiessen, Lauri Watson, Barbara Wenders, and Sharon Wiser;

Virginia Hegland, Craig Magaret, Marilyn Marston, and Jean Stook, whose editing skills and comments were invaluable to the development of this book;

Concord Fabrics (Joan Kessler Collection), for the floral fabric featured on the opening page of each chapter;

The following companies, who generously contributed the fabrics pictured on the book's pages: Hoffman California Fabrics; International Fabric Collection; P & B Textiles; Robert Kaufman Co., Inc.; and RJR Fashion Fabrics;

The Art Institute of Chicago, for the use of photographs of the Water Lilies painting by Monet;

Jane Stratton of Sunshine Crafts, for the beautiful floral arrangement;

Nancy J. Martin and the entire staff of That Patchwork Place; for cheerful answers to seemingly mundane questions and for never losing faith in two non-English-major, watercolor quiltmakers;

Each other, for sticking to deadlines, for finishing each other's thoughts, for complementing each other's ideas and skills, and for still being friends;

Abby, Lily, and Muffin, for their unconditional love.

Table of Contents

FOREWORD

Colourwash Diamonds *by Deirdre Amsden, 1987, London, England, 50½" x 51½". This quilt was inspired by the traditional pattern "Thousand Pyramids" but is executed with 60° diamonds instead of equilateral triangles. The twill weave and wool content of the fabrics contribute to the soft, muted quality of the quilt. Photo by John Coles.*

The natural world and Impressionist art clearly inspire both Pat Magaret and Donna Slusser. Their quilts reflect an evident love of gardens, colours, light, and illusion. As team teachers and coauthors, they obviously gain inspiration and approbation from one another, too.

For those who are unfamiliar with my quilts, the correlation between my own work and that of Pat and Donna needs clarification. I likewise have been influenced by the Impressionists. In particular, one vivid memory remains of being taken by my parents one grey and very wet afternoon in Paris to the Galleries de l'Orangerie to see Monet's "Water Lilies." I must have been about thirteen. We were alone in the two oval galleries, surrounded by vast paintings of water, willows, and lilies. Nothing was defined; there were only suggestions of gentle movement . . . tranquillity . . . reflections . . . the weather . . . the passage of time. The rain prevailed upon us to stay for some time in this dreamlike world.

I began making quilts in 1974 after working for fifteen years as a free-lance illustrator. From the outset, traditional, English scrap quilts and one-patch arrangements appealed to me. These preferences provided the requisite techniques when the notion of blending patches together was triggered by a gift of some Liberty of London™ Tana™ lawn offcuts. As I surveyed them in a heap on the floor, I observed how prettily the colors and patterns merged. Cutting a square from each of the fabrics, I shaded them from dark to light to make a crib quilt. To further disguise the seams, I quilted diagonally in each direction across the squares. I titled this first attempt "Colourwash," remembering an art-school exercise that required making a wash of color across the paper without blotches or tidemarks spoiling the surface. This simple concept of shading from one tone or value to another, using myriad, multicolored prints (similar to running colors into one another when painting with water-colors), forms the basis for all of my "Colourwash" quilts.

Throughout history, ideas and patterns have traversed the globe, and today's technology has accelerated this migration. Many of my quilts have received exposure in exhibitions, magazines, and books and have, in turn, occasionally influenced other quiltmakers. It is always interesting to see how others translate ideas into their own language, and it is gratifying to be given acknowledgment for innovation.

Thank you, Pat and Donna, and I wish you every success for your book, your teaching, and your future quiltmaking.

Deirdre Amsden
(England)
1992

PREFACE

Donna Ingram Slusser

Pat Maixner Magaret

Sharing is one of life's biggest and least expensive satisfactions. When we give a part of ourselves to others, the returns are multiplied. As teachers, we have gained so much from our students in terms of friendship and watching them bloom as they apply what they have learned. In turn, they have shared so much with us. We have learned that it is not worth being stingy with our ideas.

> "Flowers leave part of their fragrance in the hands that bestow them."
> ～ CHINESE PROVERB

Donna was raised in the Portland, Oregon, area. She learned to appreciate all the beauties of life: nature, art, books, music, and people. After graduating with a degree in education, she taught at the elementary school level for several years. Donna is a free spirit who enjoys all that life offers to her—family, sports (particularly baseball), animals, flowers, music, and the view from her hilltop home.

Pat came to the Northwest after being raised in Seward, Nebraska. She learned to sew doll clothes as a small child. Soon she graduated to people clothes and then on to lots of quilts. (She doesn't make clothes any more!) She earned a degree in medical technology and worked for several years. She, too, is inspired by God's green earth, enjoys her pets, art, sports (all except baseball), and watching her family grow.

We both moved to the rolling Palouse hills of eastern Washington, but at different times and for different reasons. We lived parallel lives until quilting brought us together. We soon discovered our different personalities meant we used very different techniques and methods to design and construct quilts. Pat loves graph paper, colored pencils, mathematics, and order (as in neat and tidy). Donna appears to "wing it,"

rarely uses sketches, thinks math is needed only when buying fabrics and figuring yardage, and has a sewing room with a yellow caution sign on the door. Given to her by her kids, the sign reads "This room is a Disaster Area." Pat used to complete all her projects in a timely manner until she fell under Donna's influence of putting unfinished projects in beautiful boxes with names of family and friends on them. These can either be worked on at a later date or given away. Being around Pat has taught Donna to like using templates, what the meaning of 1.414 is when figuring a diagonal line, and why a quilt is not complete until it has a label.

We've learned to encourage each other and appreciate our differences. We respect each other's creative style and the beautiful results. We are still good friends because of our common bonds, commitment to good workmanship, advocacy for excellence in quiltmaking, and love of ice cream treats.

In 1988, we were asked to teach a class at a local quilt shop. This joint effort proved to us that, despite our differences, we could develop a style based on both of our strengths. The students loved the class and appreciated being exposed to two very different approaches to almost every aspect of quiltmaking. It gave them the courage to try new ideas on their own. We've been having fun teaching quiltmaking ever since.

Donna developed a color class using 2" squares. She and her students enjoyed playing with them while doing class exercises. At home, Donna started using them to make small wall hangings and became a "2"-square addict."

Pat went through an Impressionism-appreciation stage. She collected this type of art and enjoyed researching past and contemporary artists involved with this movement. These artists quickly place unmixed daubs of paint side by side on the canvas to create a painting that looks rough and choppy up close. However, when you stand back, the eye blurs the individual elements into soft images, creating a beautiful overall effect. Some of Donna's pieces vaguely reminded Pat of Impressionism.

When we saw a photo of one of Deirdre Amsden's "colourwash quilts," we were excited to discover a quiltmaker who had successfully combined the effects of Impressionism and watercolor, using small squares. Since that time, her quilts have been our inspiration, and she is the acknowledged forerunner of this technique.

Most of our classes have a design and color orientation. The watercolor workshop was developed as a way to highlight all the effects we had been teaching. One thing leads to another. Last year when Nancy Martin, publisher, author, and knowledgeable quiltmaker, asked us to write this book, we had to decide if we could successfully integrate two strongly individual styles of writing. We've enjoyed applying the watercolor technique of "mooshing" and blending fabrics and colors to the blending of our writing styles.

We hope you will share our enthusiasm, sense of adventure, and fascination with 2" squares. Try our methods and explore ideas of your own as you discover watercolor quilts.

Pat Magaret and Donna Slusser
Pullman, Washington
1993

Pullman area quiltmakers enjoy displaying their watercolor quilt projects in the lobby outside the Museum of Art at Washington State University. (©Photo by Bill Watts, Hot Shots)

Introduction

Have you secretly dreamed of being a watercolor artist—of letting colors run together and blend effortlessly across the paper? Have you wished you could be a French Impressionist like Monet or Renoir and capture nature's beauty and the special effects of light and luminosity on canvas? Combining techniques from each of these methods has led us to making watercolor quilts.

We love scrap quilts. Why? Perhaps our attraction is due to the rich beauty produced by the interaction of many different colors and print textures, including florals, plaids, paisleys, geometrics, scenics, juveniles, and tapestries. We never lose interest in such a quilt.

Blues in the Night by Eleanor M. Cole, 1988, Pullman, Washington, 92" x 94". This is a traditional scrap quilt, where pattern is established through contrast. Eleanor's friends in Pullman made the blocks for this friendship quilt.

Hidden Garden *by Nancy Larson-Powers, 1992, Pullman, Washington, 27" x 27". A simple design is given a contemporary flavor using watercolor methods.*

Perhaps we like scrap quilts because the fabrics bring back memories of special people, special places, and good times. Perhaps it is the great fun we have integrating a wide assortment of fabrics into one work of art. Each step in the quiltmaking process allows us to touch and contemplate each fabric in our stash or scrap bag. We can include our own personal collection of favorite fabrics, memory-evoking fabrics, and in general all those fabrics that have crossed our path and have had significance in our lives.

Last but not least, perhaps the best reason we have for loving scrap quilts is because we are fabri-holics. These quilts give us a chance to showcase all those fabrics we have hoarded, traded, received as gifts, collected, and saved. They can relieve us of our guilt for buying fabric without a specific project in mind. (On second thought, we never buy fabric with nothing in mind—we are always buying for future scrap quilt projects!)

We have seen an evolution in the scrap quilt world. Until recently, the overall design was produced by creating contrasts. Lighter-colored scraps were placed next to darker-colored scraps to create a pattern. A *traditional color scheme* was often used because we were concerned with how well colors go together. These quilts, though beautiful, were static and rather flat, lacking motion and dimension.

Today, trained artists have begun to put away their paints and pick up fabrics instead. They find a blending of scraps more exciting than creating contrast. Also, when so many pieces are used, it is impossible to focus on traditional color schemes.

Instead, there emerge impressions of color, a blending of many individual pieces into a whole. Now we think in terms of *color effects*, such as light, luminosity, and movement, and we use color value as our guide. Specific colors may develop but they are secondary to the overall effect of the piece.

One such artist is Deirdre Amsden, from London, England. She is a trained artist-illustrator who now quilts and teaches. She is known for her "colourwash" series of quilts, made with her technique of using fabrics so that colors and values gradually change. This new style of scrap quilt creates suggestions of light sources within the piece. Effects, such as reflected luster and luminosity, add interest as well as dimension. It doesn't matter what colors are used. It is the light effects produced by the blending that are remembered.

> "Once your mind is stretched by a new idea, it will never again return to its original size."
>
> ~ OLIVER WENDALL HOLMES

Deirdre uses predominantly Liberty of London™ Tana™ lawn fabrics in her colorwash quilts. These cotton prints are delicate and rather subdued in appearance. Their design characteristics are different from the majority of prints available in the United States.

Because we each have different fabric sources, our quilts reflect these differences. We have expanded the watercolor concept to recreate new flowers and images, and to produce shaded landscapes as well as smeared geometric forms.

Watercolor quilts evoke emotional responses in everyone who sees them. Their moods, subtle shadings, color pockets, and soft transitions capture deep feelings and are thought provoking; a frequent comment is that these works have "life" to them.

They look deceptively simple. In fact, they are endlessly challenging. Playing with watercolor squares is addictive. If you like jigsaw puzzles and that elusive "search for the perfect piece," you will love watercolor quilts.

If your hands would rather pat and touch fabric than apply paints to canvas, this is the medium for you. Put down the paints and brushes; put away the canvas and textured paper. Get out your fabrics. Find a wall or large vertical surface that can be your new canvas. We're going to combine watercolor painting with Impressionism to create watercolor quilts.

Notice the differences between U.S.–produced prints on the left and the British-produced Liberty of London™ prints on the right.

What's Ahead

If you have not yet read the Introduction, please do so.

Watercolor Quilts is *not* a pattern book. We have arranged the information as a hands-on design process workbook and idea source. This book is based on a sequential learning process in which each step builds on previously learned information. Thus, it should be read in the order presented.

Included is information about the supplies you will need as well as some optional tools that will make the process easier.

The chapter on fabric selection emphasizes the need for a wide variety (but small quantities) of many different fabrics. This chapter is one of the most important sections in the book. It might be helpful to go to your personal fabric collection or library and find similar fabrics to compare with those shown as examples. Learn to recognize the properties of color and use the terms correctly as you work with your fabrics and projects. Identify the elements of design and different surface textures. Analyze the collection to determine where there are gaps—where certain types of fabrics are missing. Most quiltmakers find at least two or three areas where they need to add more fabrics. A comprehensive fabric collection made up of good-quality prints is an absolute necessity and eases the frustration level when actually working on a watercolor piece. A small wall quilt often includes over two hundred different fabrics, so start collecting now.

Preparing the fabric for cutting is another important part of this chapter.

The chapter on cutting shows you how to cut your prepared fabrics into 2" squares. The process of sorting fabrics by value is one that takes practice to perfect. We share tips for making it easy. Once you feel comfortable with sorting, watercolor quilts will be a snap. We show you how to put the many pieces together to create your watercolor quilt. We know you will become so engrossed in the process that supper will be late, and you will often find yourself analyzing people's clothing to see how it would look if cut into 2" squares. Your slogan will be "Watercolor forever; housework never."

Once your project is designed, you'll find tips on how to sew it together. Border selection, backing options, quilting designs, and signing your work of art are also covered.

After reading through the book for the first time, study the photographs and examine the illustrations, analyzing the various color and value changes in each one. Take some time to let all the information soak in. Creativity cannot be rushed. Practice the shading exercises illustrated in the book. Select a simple design for a beginning watercolor project. This just might be the beginning of your "watercolor era." You, too, may discover that you have become a "2"-square addict."

This type of watercolor does not require brushes, palettes, or paper. Though we, too, are artists, our tools are of a different nature.

Tools of the Trade

Adequate lighting

Steam iron

Gridded vertical design wall

Sewing machine

Pressing surface

Eraser

Pencils

Cotton thread

Fabric scissors

Small scissors

Graph paper, ¼" grid

Tracing paper

Reducing glass

Pins

6" x 24" clear ruler

Rotary cutter

Cutting mat

6" x 6" clear ruler

Ruby Beholder™

PLANNING TOOLS

Graph Paper: Use graph paper to draft a plan or map of your project. Since you will not be using this paper for template making, the accuracy of the grid is not of the utmost importance. Inexpensive graph paper works fine.

Tracing Paper: Lightweight, see-through tracing paper is handy for creating numerous shadings without disturbing the original line drawing.

Pencils: We prefer .5mm mechanical pencils. The point is always sharp so you don't waste time looking for a pencil sharpener.

Eraser: Where there is a pencil, there had better be a good eraser. We prefer the soft white or gum variety. They smudge less and do not discolor your paper. Sometimes this type of eraser will even remove accidental pencil marks from fabric.

CUTTING TOOLS

Rotary Cutter and Extra Blades: Rotary cutters are available in both large and small sizes. We prefer the large wheel as it seems to work the best for general, all-purpose cutting. Experiment and choose whichever works best for you.

Cutting Mat: Cutting mats with self-healing surfaces are available in a variety of sizes. Purchase the largest one you can afford for general cutting purposes, at least 18" x 24". We also like the smaller, more portable 12" x 18" size for taking to classes and to use in front of the TV or in the family room.

Acrylic Rotary Ruler: Sturdy, accurate rulers are a must for rotary cutting. They come in a variety of sizes. A large 6" x 24" ruler is necessary for general cutting. A smaller 6" square works great for slicing strips into 2" squares. Even though an inch is an inch, there is sometimes a slight variation between the measurement increments of different brands of rulers. When purchasing multiple rulers, it might be a good idea to buy the same brand, assuming they will be consistent.

Scissors: Use scissors for snipping threads during the construction process.

DESIGNING TOOLS

Vertical Design Wall: When designing any quilt, it is much easier to see the design develop if viewed on a vertical plane (the wall) rather than on a horizontal plane (tabletop or floor). Your quilt squares will cling to a large piece (minimum size 36" x 45") of white needlepunch, such as Pellon™ fleece or Thermo-Lam™, or white flannel mounted on the wall. (Felt does not work quite as well.) Tape it to the wall as a temporary surface or stretch it over Celotex™ or sound board (available at building supply stores) for a more permanent arrangement. We have found that designing is easier if you mark a 4" grid over the surface of this design wall with a permanent marker. Pretest the marker on a corner or the reverse side of the surface. This grid gives you a framework on which to build your design. A premarked working wall is available by mail order. See Sources, page 110.

Reducing Glass: This tool looks like a magnifying glass, but instead of enlarging, it reduces the image. This allows you to get farther away from your quilt, even in a small work area, so you can see your developing design from a different perspective. Projects look as they will appear once they are sewn together. Problem areas jump out and solutions become more evident. A reducing glass can be purchased at art supply stores and some quilt shops. This tool is optional but well worth the money. Instead of a reducing glass, you can get the same effect by looking through the wrong end of binoculars, or through the viewfinder of your camera. Those peepholes you put in your door for security purposes also reduce images, but at the same time they distort them slightly.

Value Finder: This tool is not necessary but is very helpful. Looking through this piece of red acrylic or acetate eliminates all colors in the fabric so all you see is value (the lightness or darkness of the fabric). This tool helps when sorting fabrics and working on your design. It, however, does not work as well with the red color family. Red cloud filters for photography also work.

Window Template: This tool is particularly helpful when looking at exciting fabric designs to see how they will look when cut and sewn. Directions for making your own window template are on page 21.

Ruby Beholder: This tool has a value finder on one end and a 1½" window template on the other end.

Polaroid™ Camera: It is helpful to photograph projects in process. If you make changes in your design, you can refer to the photos to see which way you liked it best. This tool is optional but very helpful.

Good Lighting: Probably the most important tool you need is good lighting. It not only makes the designing process easier but is also essential for a satisfactory end product. The best light source is good, indirect daylight because all colors will look true. If investing in artificial light for your work area, consider full-spectrum or daylight fluorescent lighting. It is the next best thing to "Mother Nature." A combination of fluorescent and incandescent lighting is also a good alternative for approximating natural daylight.

Gift Wrap Tissue Paper: If your design needs to be moved while it is in progress, it will take forever to pin each square in place on the design-wall fleece. The following method seems implausible but it really works.

1. Pin sheets of tissue paper securely to the design, using approximately 10-12 pins for each sheet.

2. Roll the tissue paper, design, and working wall from the bottom to the top very carefully. Pin securely.

3. When unrolling the design, ask another person to help you secure it to the top of the board or wall and carefully unroll the piece. Remove the tissue paper and continue working on the project.

CONSTRUCTION TOOLS

Sewing Machine

Use any straight-stitch machine. To make sure your seam allowances are exactly ¼" wide, see page 96. Some people choose to use an even-feed foot all the time to prevent slippage. However, it is not necessary. We have found it is always best to use the same machine while working on an individual project. We often look at the stitching from different angles on different machines. Or, the seam allowance varies just enough from machine to machine to make a difference that is very noticeable when trying to match seams. (Pat has two Singer Featherweight sewing machines. She has calibrated the ¼" mark on each of them, and yet, the finished seam allowances are different when she uses both machines for a single project.)

Thread: We prefer 100% cotton, general sewing thread. Use neutral colors that will blend with all colors of fabrics. Use light thread for light fabrics and dark thread for dark fabrics. We use lots of grays and tans.

Iron and Pressing Surface: A good steam iron is invaluable for producing quality workmanship. We use a dry iron when pressing seams right after stitching. We find that using steam at this point causes stretching of the raw edges that are not yet sewn. When your quilt top is finished, give it a good press with a steam iron. To save steps, locate a smaller pressing board close to your machine.

Rolling Secretarial Chair: It is great to be able to roll from the sewing machine, to the design wall, to the pressing center. This tool is nice but not necessary.

Fabric: How could we forget? You will need lots of it. In fact, you might want to take a break and go down to your local quilt shop or sewing center right now. But first, read the next chapter.

Fabric Selection & Preparation

All artists work with color. A painter is able to mix the colors as desired on a palette. The canvas and paper, as well as the brush strokes, give needed texture. Quilters, however, rely upon the designs and color already built into the fabric surface for texture. Their palette is determined by searching, collecting, hoarding, and trading available fabrics.

Our choices are unlimited. Using many different prints adds richness to our quilts. The designs of different fabrics work together beautifully when placed side by side.

When choosing a color scheme and fabrics for a traditional quilt design, quilters go through a process of addition and elimination by putting together various combinations of colors and fabrics. They add and subtract bolts and pieces of fabric until a final few are chosen. During the process, the color scheme is uppermost in their minds.

To create a watercolor quilt, you must learn to work in a different way. Subtle gradations of value and color changes are used to create special color effects. Instead of thinking about color when selecting fabrics, you must concentrate on value.

Here are some basic terms you'll need to understand so you can apply them to your fabric collection.

COLOR AND ITS PROPERTIES

Hue is the name of a color or color family that we see in the images on fabric surfaces. Hue names include red, yellow, blue, orange, green, and purple. Sometimes, one hue or color will predominate. Other times, more than one, or many, colors are combined to make up the surface design. Such a print is called multicolored. We prefer to use a wide variety of multicolored prints in watercolor quilts.

Value is the lightness or darkness of the colored surface. There is an infinite number of degrees of value between very, very dark and very, very light within each color family. Even multicolored prints have value (light, medium, or dark). When you place two fabrics of different values next to each other, one will be lighter than the other. However, when you add a still lighter fabric to the group, what was once the lightest fabric becomes a medium-value color. Value is relative. The value of a color depends upon the value of the colors that surround it.

Value in fabrics: light, medium, dark

Intensity is the dullness or brightness of a color. Some fabrics have more pure color in their print than others. If a color is very pure, it is very intense. If a color is dull (or "grayed" or looks muddy), gray or another color (its complement) has been added to make it less intense. Adding white or black does not make a color less intense; it simply changes the value. Dark, medium, and light colors can each be very pure and intense, or very dull. Intensity is relative. It also depends on the intensity of the fabrics that surround it.

Intensity in fabrics: bright and dull

PRINT DESIGN ELEMENTS

Scale describes the size of the motif in the surface design. Sometimes motifs are very small and sometimes they are quite large. Generally speaking, small prints do not work well in watercolor quilts. They tend to be static, and their designs do not flow into neighboring squares. Medium- to large-scale prints work best for watercolor quilts.

Scale in fabrics (size of motifs): small, medium, large

Line describes a mark or stroke. The design elements printed on the fabric are made up of colors and lines. Together they can make a recognizable shape, such as a flower, leaf, or animal. When large-scale prints are cut up into small pieces, the original design element or motif (flower, leaf) is often lost. Only color and lines are left.

After cutting, squares may contain no complete motif—only color and lines.

Contrast occurs when there is a variety of differences in value, color, intensity, and line within a print. If the differences are minimal, the print is considered low contrast. When differences are more readily apparent, it is high contrast.

Great for watercolor!   *Save for other projects.*

Symmetry refers to even or uneven distribution of color properties and design elements across the print. Asymmetrical prints (uneven distribution of motifs and colors) are better choices than symmetrical prints in watercolor quilts. *Save for other projects.*

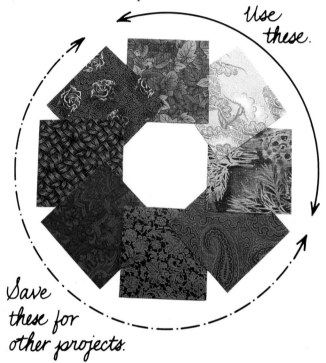

Great for watercolor projects!

In summary, fabrics used in watercolor quilts should have:
- ❧ different colors
- ❧ contrasting values and intensities
- ❧ a variety of scales
- ❧ asymmetrical lines and design

SURFACE TEXTURE OR DESIGN

Color, color properties, and design elements combine to form surface texture or surface design, which means we are actually talking about how a fabric looks. Sometimes, a fabric may evoke a message in our brain as to how the surface would feel if we were to touch it.

Let's consider some aspects and types of surface texture and their application in watercolor quilts.

Monochromatic Prints

When a print is made up of a variety of values, all in the same color family, it is a monochromatic print. Sometimes there is high contrast between the values, and good design lines are also present. These can be used in watercolor quilts.

Use these.

Save these for other projects.

At other times, there will be little contrast between the values. These monochromatic prints will appear as a solid color when viewed from ten feet (or more) away. They are also called tone-on-tone prints. As a general rule, these do not work well in watercolor quilts. However, if they are very dark or very light and contain some good lines, they can be used. The dark areas of the watercolor quilts imply shade or shadow. The light areas imply bright-light sources or reflected light. Think about how things look when they are in the dark or if they are in a shadow. You do not see much change of color or much detail. Think about how something looks when viewed in a bright light. Sometimes our eyes water and sting and maybe we even squint. Again, we do not see much contrast in value.

Experience has taught us that only a few of the darkest darks and lightest lights should be used in a watercolor design. You will need only a few of these in your watercolor fabric collection.

Multicolored Prints

Most of the prints in watercolor quilts should come from this category. You will find a variety of different textures and designs. Medium- to large-scale prints work best. When they are cut up and placed side by side with other similar prints, the boundaries between the pieces dissolve. Squares with shared colors run and blur together. Squares with shared lines blend together.

The following multicolored textures and designs are fun to use in watercolor quilts!

Florals—The most common motif to be found in prints consists of flowers. Some are realistic while others are stylized.

Paisleys—These decorative, curled teardrop patterns are inspired by the designs in woolen shawls woven and produced in Paisley, Scotland, during the 1800s.

Geometrics—These designs are based on all those old familiar shapes we studied in high school geometry class: squares and lines (plaids and stripes), triangles and circles. Medium- to large-scale plaids, especially if they are unbalanced (asymmetrical), work well in watercolor quilts. Simple stripes will not flow in a watercolor piece. However, a more elaborate, decorative border stripe works fine.

Theme Prints—Look for the following: fruits and vegetables; animals, birds and fish; people; scenics; juveniles; tropicals; tapestries; ethnic prints (including Japanese prints, African prints, and Indonesian batiks); textures with the look of wood, water, and marble.

When selecting fabrics for a watercolor quilt, it is important to keep in mind all of the above information on color, properties of color, design elements, and surface textures. Look for fabrics with motion, with lines that move the eye. Look for fabrics that set a mood, for example, soft and swirly, or sharp and agitating. These can be used to create certain effects in specific areas of the quilt.

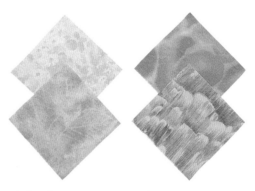

Look for fantastic prints. These are prints that you will use in almost every quilt you make. They go with everything because they contain many colors, have good value characteristics, and feature great lines. We will each have our own unique set of fantastic prints. They will not be the same for everyone.

Generally speaking, think about how a fabric will look when cut into 2" squares.

- ❧ Will all the squares look alike? If so, this fabric is probably too symmetrical for watercolor quilts.
- ❧ Will all the squares look different? If so, this fabric will probably work fine.

To help you visualize how a fabric will look after being cut into small squares and then sewn together, make and use a window template. This tool gives you a window for visualization that can also be used later to plan and cut out specific motifs or to identify the location of specific lines and colors.

To make a window template:

1. Draw a square, 1½" x 1½", on posterboard or plastic template material.
2. Add ¼"-wide seam allowances to all sides to make a new second outer square, 2" x 2".
3. Cut out on both sets of lines.

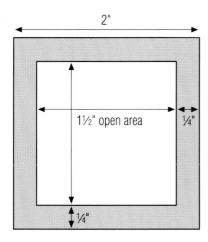

ORGANIZING YOUR PERSONAL FABRIC LIBRARY

The best fiber content to use in your watercolor quilts is 100% cotton. It is durable, handles well, and is easy care. If you use 100% cottons exclusively, all the fabrics in your quilts will age at the same rate. For example, cotton-polyester blends tend to last longer than cotton, and silk disintegrates more quickly.

We both store our fabric collections in an organized fashion on shelves. Actually, Pat's fabrics are stored in an organized fashion, and Donna's are stored in an organized mess!

We both love to read and discovered that we were thinking of our fabric collections as libraries. Individual fabrics, like books, have a lot of variety. They, too, can be categorized into sections because of certain similarities. Our fabrics are grouped by color and design type—plaids and stripes, juvenile and youth, theme prints and favorites.

As you organize your fabrics, make note of the fabric deficiencies in your collection and ask yourself the following questions:

1. Do I tend to collect certain colors and avoid others?
2. Do I have a predominance of lights or darks or medium values?
3. Do I have a balance of different-size prints?
4. Are most of my fabrics dull or bright?
5. Do I have an assortment of prints that read as different surface textures?

To have a complete fabric library, you need a large variety of prints. *Don't just collect fabrics you like, but collect those you need.*

You will need small quantities of a large variety of medium- to large-scale prints—all colors, all values, all intensities, and all textures. You may find yourself using hundreds of different prints in one quilt. Also notice the back side of each fabric. Sometimes the reverse side works well to achieve a slightly lighter and more diffuse image. Because so many fabrics are used in one watercolor quilt, it serves as a statement and document of the fabrics available in our times.

EXPANDING YOUR FABRIC LIBRARY

As you search for new fabrics to add to your collection, support your local quilt shops and fabric stores. They have all the latest colors and designs from which to choose. Ask for small quantities of many different prints. Some shops even have an assortment of precut fabrics in small packages available for mail order. See Sources on page 110. It is not necessary to purchase large amounts of any one fabric. A fat quarter (an 18" x 22" piece) is usually sufficient. Purchase more if it is a favorite print or one that you will use often.

In addition, there are many mail-order fabric clubs you can join. Periodically, they send you packets of swatches to consider purchasing. These swatches are usually 4" or 6" squares and some are great to cut into the watercolor squares.

When looking for fabrics to add to your fabric library, try to find the same print in different colorways (different color combinations). It is great fun to find them all in one quilt.

Do you have a mini-collection of fabrics with a particular theme, such as Christmas prints, vegetable and fruit motifs, or fish prints? Continue searching for more of these fabrics and see how many different ones you can use in one quilt.

Look for ordinary as well as unique prints. It is fun to put natural combinations together in a quilt, such as placing a bunny motif near a vegetable print or a cat's head amidst florals. Or, position a fish's eye down in a leafy area or a penguin print next to a palm tree, just for the fun of it all.

Whimsical motifs are fun to hide in your quilts. Small bits and pieces of special fabrics can bring wonderful memories to mind.

Quilters are notorious for saving even the smallest pieces of fabric left over from all their sewing projects. Remember, these scraps are part of your library. Watercolor quilts are memory quilts. Happy memories of mother are conjured up when you see the fabric from her Easter dress of 1947. Plaids and prints from family clothing recall a graduation dress or a Father's Day shirt. The summer vacation to the British Isles comes to mind when you see those Liberty of London prints and Scottish plaids that you brought back as souvenirs. It is amazing how one small square of fabric allows you to visualize the whole bolt, the whole dress or shirt, or to remember a special event.

You can add to your fabric library by trading or exchanging fabrics with your quilt-guild members or among your quilting friends. One simple method of expanding your watercolor fabric collection is to get seven friends together for a fabric exchange. Ask each person to bring seventy 6" squares. To prepare for the exchange, assign each person a different color family. Ask each one to select ten different prints within their color family and to cut a 6" x 42" strip from each fabric; then crosscut it into 6" squares. There will be seven squares from each of ten fabrics for a total of seventy squares to exchange.

On the day of the exchange, find a good-sized table and move it to the center of the room. Have each participant place her stack of seventy squares near the edge of the table. Then the fun begins. Invite everyone to pour themselves a glass of their favorite beverage (or provide Quilters' Tea made from the recipe that follows) while you turn on some music for atmosphere. If you want the exchange to last all afternoon, perhaps a sonata selection will do. If you want to get the exchange completed quickly (so you can get started on your watercolor quilt), a lively array of John Philip Sousa's marches might be more appropriate.

As you enjoy each other's company and admire and touch the fabric, go around the table picking up one square from each pile until they are gone. Everyone should end up with seventy different fabrics and fond memories of a fun afternoon. You may have other good ideas for fabric exchanges.

Watercolor quilts can be friendship quilts, too.

Quilters' Tea

Hunt through your scraps and find a piece of discarded muslin (approximately 12" x 12") to use as a spice bag. Wash the fabric thoroughly and tie the following ingredients in it:

9 small tea bags, tags removed
2 cinnamon sticks
10 whole allspice
peel from half an orange, cut into strips

Place 11 cups water in a saucepan. Add spice bag, bring to a boil, and simmer 10 minutes. Add the following ingredients and simmer 1 additional minute:

one 12-oz. can frozen orange juice concentrate,
    undiluted and thawed
½ cup lemon juice
½ cup sugar
⅓ cup honey
Remove spice bag and serve to 12–15 thirsty quilters.

FABRIC PREPARATION

It is important to prepare and process your fabrics for colorfastness and shrinkage before they are cut into the squares for a watercolor quilt. For colorfastness, test each piece, using our method or one of your own. To preshrink fabrics, wash and dry them, using the method that works best for you.

How We Prepare Our Fabrics

1. Test for colorfastness by snipping off a small piece of each fabric; wet snippet thoroughly. Do not squeeze out excess water; place on a white paper towel and let dry. Remove from paper towel to see if any dye transferred to the towel.
2. If not colorfast, process fabric with color-setting agents (vinegar, salt) and test again for colorfastness. If the fabric is still not colorfast, discard.
3. Wash and dry fabric. Iron if necessary.
4. Cut a 2"-wide strip across the width (42"–45") of each fabric.
5. Cut the 2"-wide strip into 2" squares.
6. Fold and store larger pieces of fabric until needed.

Using pretested and preshrunk fabric is our preference for all our quiltmaking projects. But, occasionally, a few unprocessed squares will find their way into our pieces. How will this affect the finished project? And what about using the unprocessed, precut 2" squares sold in quilt shops and through mail-order sources? Processing several hundred 2" squares is a monumental task! Remember that the majority of the watercolor quilts will be wall quilts and will not be laundered as frequently as other quilted projects. If special cleaning care is given to a quilt that has both processed and unprocessed fabrics in it, we find that serious bleeding is eliminated and uneven shrinkage is reduced.

When your fabrics are processed, it is time to cut them into 2" squares. Get ready, get set, cut!

Cutting & Sorting Fabric Squares

CUTTING

After you have collected and processed a wide assortment of fabrics, they must be cut into 2" squares.

The size of the squares is very important. We find that 2" squares of fabric (unfinished size) work best. They are easily blurred by the eye to produce a smooth flow of color and light when viewed across an average-size room. The larger the size of the squares, the farther back you must stand so your eyes flow easily across the piece.

Accuracy is the name of this game. Use accurate rulers and be sure the blade in your rotary cutter is sharp. Use rotary-cutting tools to cut a 2"-wide strip across each piece of fabric. Cut this fabric strip into 2" squares.

To cut squares:

1. Fold the fabric in half, selvage to selvage. Make sure the fold is nearest you, the selvages farthest away, and the uneven edges on the left. (Reverse these techniques if you are left-handed.) Line up one edge of a 6" square ruler with the fold of the fabric. Place a 6" x 24" ruler to the left of the 6" square.

2. Remove the 6" square ruler and use the rotary cutter to cut along the right edge of the ruler. Hold the ruler in place by pressing downward with the left hand, spreading fingers wide. Sometimes it helps to stabilize the ruler by placing your little finger on the fabric next to the ruler. Push the rotary cutter away from yourself with even, downward pressure. Move your fingers along the ruler to keep it from shifting or moving. This cut edge is now straight.

3. Slide the ruler to the right and line up the vertical line that measures 2" from the original cut. Also align one of the horizontal lines near the bottom of the ruler with the fold of the fabric. Cut along the right edge of the ruler to make a strip that is 2" wide.

4. Use the 6" square to cut 2" squares. Align the top and bottom edges of the strip with the horizontal lines and the left edge of the fabric with the vertical line.

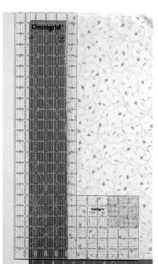
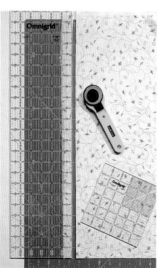
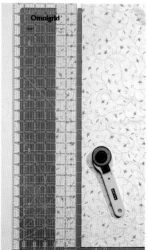
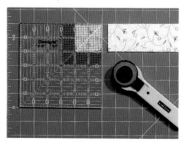

When using this method of random cutting, particularly on fabric that has an unevenly distributed pattern (asymmetrical), you may have some squares that have little or no motif on them. Put these in a discard pile to be used in projects other than watercolor quilts.

It is a lot of fun to cut the fabric into strips and squares. You get to touch the fabrics several more times and see how the colors, lines, motifs, and designs look when you have only a small part of the original design. Interesting things happen. Maybe you get only part of the french fries or ice cream cone from a junk-food print—or only a big fish eye from a watery print. Look at that square that has only the tiger's whiskers and nose. And what about the people print where you see only a hand or arm or part of the head? These are wonderful to include in your project.

Random cutting often shows only part of a print. Enjoy!

We each have special fabrics we like to include in the watercolor quilts we make. We each look for prints that reflect our family's interests. Donna is a musician, loves to work in her flower and vegetable gardens, raises bunnies, watches hummingbirds, and is a baseball addict. Her husband and kids are golfers and have pet dogs and cats. Her husband also paints, fishes, and raises chickens. One son hunts and fishes, another son is in the Air Force (airplanes), and her daughter loves strawberries. Pat, on the other hand, keeps her eyes open for chocolate motifs, sunflowers, pansies, and jogging prints. Her husband collects stamps, hunts game birds, and watches and feeds birds. She hunts for outdoor themes and USA prints for one son, reptile-texture prints for another son, and fashion or dance motifs for her daughter. The new puppy is remembered with a special print of dog motifs.

You will find that looking for your special prints in shops is lots of fun and that family members like to play detective to find their squares in the finished quilt.

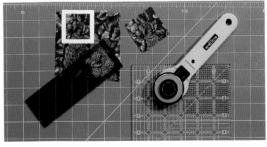

These prints reflect the interests of the authors and their families. Use a window template or the window template in the Ruby Beholder tool to cut specific 2" squares.

Rather than randomly cutting these special fabrics, you may want to use the Ruby Beholder or a window template (described on page 16) to see exactly what your special motif will look like when cut and sewn.

There may be a little waste when using either the random method or when cutting out special motifs. Save these scraps for other quilting projects. Occasionally, while you are working on the watercolor design, you may need to cut a specific square to go into a spot, to create the special effect you want. Use the Ruby Beholder or the window template to find the perfect square.

Cutting the fabrics into 2" squares is another area where we each use our own methods. Pat cuts only one fabric at a time. Donna cuts multiple layers but then has to sort the fabrics into individual piles that contain only one fabric. Choose the method that works best for you. Be sure to take frequent breaks when cutting to relieve pressure and tension on the shoulders, arms, and wrists.

During the cutting process, you are fracturing the design elements and motifs of the surface pattern. Each square will now be a combination of colors and lines. These will be your palette for painting a watercolor quilt.

SORTING

Once your fabrics have been selected, prepared, and cut into 2" squares, it is time to arrange and sort them. The traditional method of sorting quilt fabrics is to use color families as a guide—blue piles, red piles, yellow piles, for example. However, coordinating colors is *not* the method used to achieve the watercolor effect. Instead, you will need to sort your fabrics by value. If your fabric library is extensive, you may want to sort by value within each color family.

It will be helpful to review the short section on color and its properties on pages 17–18 at this time. A value scale has gradations in order from light to dark.

This value scale pays no particular attention to color. It uses subtle shadings of dark, medium, and light values to blend and achieve the smooth flow of gradations. In order to sort the fabrics by value, use the following six categories.

- dark Darks . . . . light Darks
- dark Mediums . . . . light Mediums
- dark Lights . . . . light Lights

The photographs on page 27 illustrate sorting fabrics by value, using these six categories.

Begin sorting your squares by value, placing them in the correct row. It is a game of comparison to see where the fabrics blend in the best. As you add squares to each row, overlap them slightly so you can compare each new addition with what has already been sorted. Remember, value is relative. Use your reducing tool and value finder. Stand back and squint. Look at each row to see if any squares jump out at you. Are they too dark or too light? Move them to a different row and see if they fit in better.

Some prints will not fit neatly into any row. Place them in the row where they appear to blend in the best. You can always move them again.

Remember to consider all the values within each square. Some large-scale prints will have many value changes within them. When cut into small squares, some squares from the same fabric will fit into several different value rows. Sort these squares and place them in the appropriate rows.

Large-scale prints may have squares of different values when cut.

A value scale shows gradations from light to dark, using watercolor fabric squares.

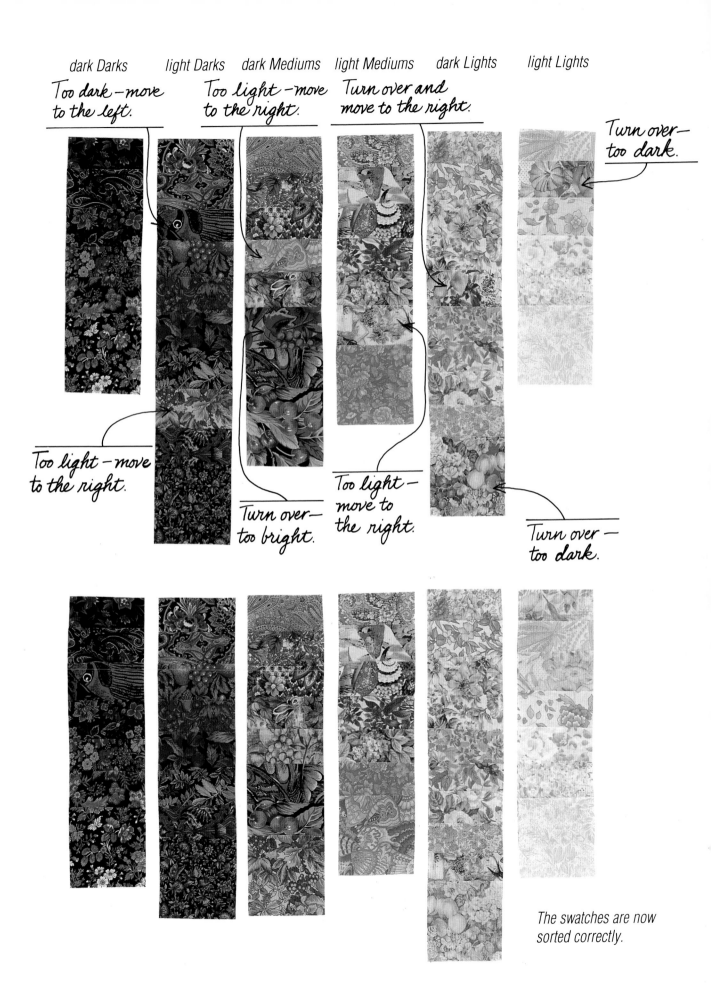

dark Darks   light Darks   dark Mediums   light Mediums   dark Lights   light Lights

Too dark — move to the left.

Too light — move to the right.

Turn over and move to the right.

Turn over — too dark.

Too light — move to the right.

Turn over — too bright.

Too light — move to the right.

Turn over — too dark.

The swatches are now sorted correctly.

Fabrics with light backgrounds will not necessarily fit into the lighter rows. Fabrics with dark backgrounds will not necessarily fit into the darker rows. Very high-contrast fabrics, for example, dark green leaves on a white background, can be difficult to use. Turn them over and check the back side. If the image is more diffuse and the contrast less extreme, sort these pieces using the back side as the "right" side.

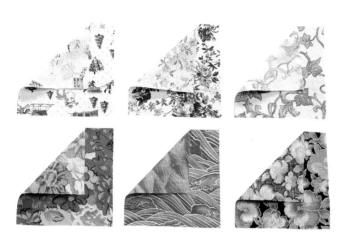

Back sides give softer images when fabrics have high-contrast prints. Back sides of bright fabrics may have a softer effect.

If some fabrics seem too bright, they, too, can be used on the back side.

We have often used the back side of many fabrics in our quilts to achieve a softer, muted effect. Some of our students have a difficult time using the back side of the fabric. Most of us have not been encouraged to use the special properties of the back side of fabric, but sometimes you will find the back side of a fabric is just what you need to complete a row. However, because the dyes soak through unevenly on the back side of some fabrics, you will not be able to use all fabrics in this manner. Always check both sides of the fabric when sorting watercolor fabrics. Another solution to subduing fabrics that are too bright and those that have too much contrast is to try overdyeing them, using a strong tea solution or Procion MX dyes.

As you sort, make a separate pile for squares that will not work in a watercolor quilt. These include fabrics that look like a solid color, those that have too much

contrast and will not work on the back side, and the shocking brights that can't be tamed. Use these pieces in other projects. Check "Fabric Selection," beginning on page 17, for help in identifying these fabrics and understanding why they don't work in watercolor projects.

When you have finished sorting half of the squares, walk away from them with your back turned. Give your eyes a rest by looking at other objects in the room, or take a break. When you come back, stand six to eight feet away from the sorted fabrics. Squint and use a reducing tool and value finder or the Ruby Beholder to look at the rows. You will be amazed to see the fabrics already blending and beginning to look like a watercolor piece! Continue sorting, working quickly.

When the sorting is finished, double-check each row. Does any print stop the eye from moving smoothly down the row of squares? If so, remove it and check the row again. Is the flow better now?

After sorting, you will have a better feeling about where the strengths and weaknesses are in your 2" fabric collection. Maybe you are low in lights and heavy in darks. Fill in the deficiencies by trading with friends or by visiting your favorite quilt shop.

There are several methods for storing the squares. Make an effort to keep the like values together. They are your palette when you begin the watercolor designing process. As new fabrics come into your possession, file them in the appropriate value file.

Pat stores her 2" squares in trays made from pizza boxes. To store yours this way, ask for large boxes at your local pizza parlor. Sometimes there is a nominal charge, but if you are a regular customer, perhaps you will get them free. Pat splits them in half at the hinged side and then slits each corner. Each box yields two trays that stack nicely.

Donna uses the cardboard boxes that hold twenty-four soda pop cans. They are sturdy with 2" sides. Ask for them at your local grocery store before they crunch them up in the recycling machine. Stack them, alternating length and width. These boxes take up more room than pizza boxes but have higher sides.

FIRST, MAKE A ROAD MAP

Watercolor quilts do not require quilt patterns in the traditional sense of the word. Therefore, it is important to have some type of design that can be used as a road map as you work on your piece.

Some artists are able to visualize exactly what they want to create without drawings or sketches in hand. (Donna tends to belong to this school.) Others find that these mental images are more difficult to evoke. (Pat is one of these poor souls.) If you find you are a visualizer, you probably will not need to spend much time with pencil and paper. Nonvisualizers can fill up a wastepaper basket before coming up with the perfect plan that can be executed. Of course, there are those who successfully use a combination of these techniques.

Whether a mental image or sketch pad is the design source, you need a plan or a road map to get from inspiration to the actual quilt itself. Your first watercolor quilt will be made entirely of fabric squares. Graph paper is perfect for planning the road map. Each small square on the paper can represent one square of fabric in the finished quilt.

Using a regular pencil, start by outlining a square that is 15 squares x 15 squares. Using the side of the pencil, gradually fill in this large square, shading from very light, through medium values, to darker values. The shading can be on the diagonal, horizontal, or vertical. It can be sketchy. Do not shade each small square individually. (Remember, you are creating an "impression.")

The shading can be horizontal.

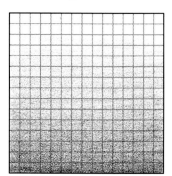

The shading can be vertical.

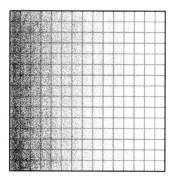

The shading can be diagonal.

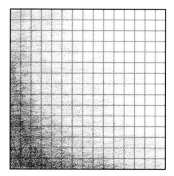

Next, outline a rectangle, 10 squares x 20 squares. Shade it from light to dark on the horizontal, vertical, or diagonal.

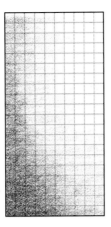

Try a shading that is dark in the corners and light in the center.

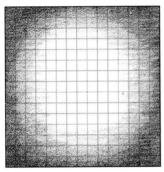

Start with two dark corners that are opposite each other. Keep the other corners light. Work toward a medium value in the center.

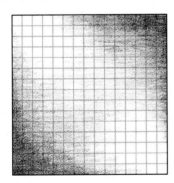

Make three bars, side by side, each 4 squares x 15 squares. Shade each bar from light to dark, making each neighboring bar the opposite of the one next to it.

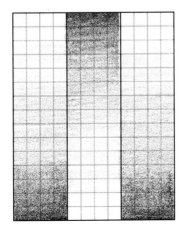

Lengthen the bars. Shade from light through medium, to dark, and back again to medium and light. As before, reverse the shading in the neighboring bar.

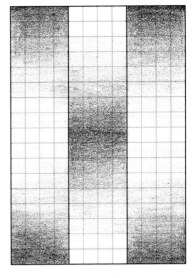

See how one idea leads to another? Many ideas start to develop. In the beginning, you will need to practice the shading techniques, using simple shapes. When you feel confident with this initial step, take the shaded squares and rectangles to the photocopy shop and make numerous copies of each. Cut out these shapes, move them around, rearrange them, and play with them. Stack them, overlap them. See if they produce secondary designs when put together—hearts, interlocking rings, or over-and-under weavings, for example.

You may wish to introduce triangles into your design in order to create some diagonal lines. For design ideas using triangles, study the photos in this book.

You can use squares with contrasting values to create diagonal or curving lines so that piecing individual squares is not necessary. See page 42. The curved lines of the heart in Donna's "Heart's Delight" on page 72 are all achieved with squares that contain contrasting values; no extra piecing was involved.

As you do these sketches and exercises, you will find combinations of shapes that please you. Save these by gluing them to a piece of paper and using them as design ideas for future projects.

Study the shadings shown for some of the quilts pictured in this book.

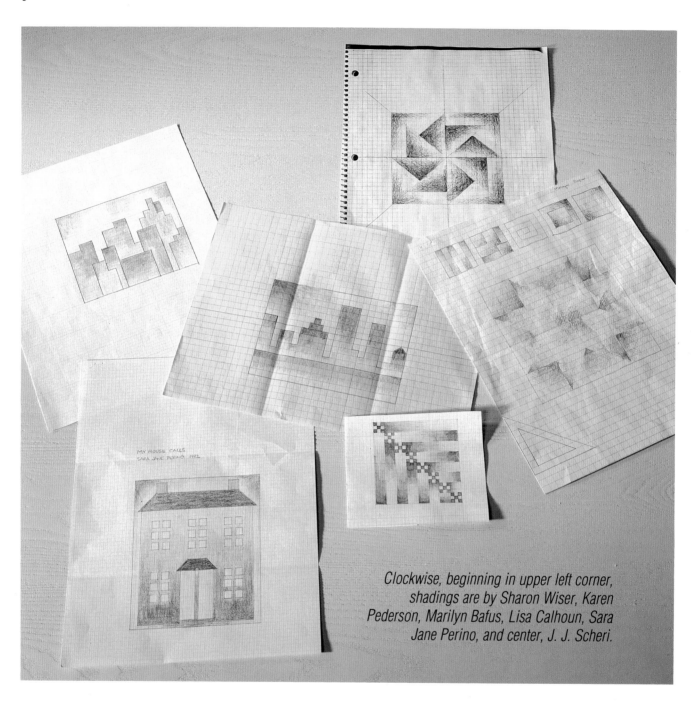

Clockwise, beginning in upper left corner, shadings are by Sharon Wiser, Karen Pederson, Marilyn Bafus, Lisa Calhoun, Sara Jane Perino, and center, J. J. Scheri.

Look at photographs of the quilts and the illustrations, examining their basic designs. Let them stir your imagination and encourage creativity. *Creativity will not happen overnight and cannot be rushed.*

For your first watercolor quilt, choose one of the simple shadings, perhaps bars or a shaded square or rectangle. Use this design to learn the various techniques needed to create a watercolor quilt. Then expand your horizons and try something more elaborate. Many of the quilts pictured in this book were created by quiltmakers after they had made only one simple watercolor quilt.

When you have your shading or design road map ready, tack it to the corner of your design wall and get ready to take the trip of a lifetime.

TAKE THE TRIP OF A LIFETIME

It's time to pack and get ready to go. Your map is close at hand and the road (the design wall) is waiting ahead of you. Assemble everything you need. Locate the sorted fabric squares close to the design wall. Clean and polish the reducing tool and value finder. Perhaps you might need a tall, cold drink and plate of fresh fruit in season (Donna's preference) or a chocolate mousse (Pat's contribution) for energy. However, we doubt you will take time to savor them because once you get going, it is hard to turn off that motor. Soft music, classical favorites, or the latest CD help set the mood.

Start your engines and let's travel to the land of watercolor and Impressionism.

The watercolor artist, working with paints and pigments on textured paper, must work quickly since this is a fast medium. The colors "run" or smear because water is added to the paint. Broad washes of bold or delicate colors are laid down with dizzying speed. Loose forms and suggestive shapes are painted while the paper is wet. If details and distinct edges are desired, they are often added after the paper is dry.

In essence, we are watercolor and Impressionist painters. Our paints are small fabric squares. We, too, will be working quickly. Obviously, water can't be added to our paints (fabrics) to achieve the "running" and "smearing" effect. Instead, we borrow a method from the French Impressionists, such as Monet and Renoir, who lived in the last quarter of the nineteenth century. They worked in much the same way, quickly placing unmixed daubs of paint on their canvas, side by side. The finished paintings are beautiful because the eye, with the aid of distance, blurs these specks of color into a coordinated composition. These works capture special effects of nature—light, luminosity, and luster. Up close, a watercolor quilt looks like a jumbled-up scrap quilt gone wild, but when you stand back, you see the squares blended into exciting effects.

The graded wash below was painted by Lloyd Slusser with dark at one end and light at the other.

He dropped water on the painted watercolor surface and tipped the paper to create runs, smears, and subtle patterns.

Lloyd used two colors with dark at the outer edges and a blending effect in the center to create this graded wash.

Monet's Water Lilies *(Art Institute of Chicago)*
The lily pond is beautiful from a distance . . .
(Water Lilies, 1906, oil on canvas, 87.6cm x 92.7cm,
Mr. and Mrs. Martin A. Ryerson Collection, 1933.1157,
©The Art Institute of Chicago)

. . . but the blossoms only look like
brush strokes of paint when seen up close.

Lifting Fog *by Patricia Maixner Magaret, 1991, Pullman, Washington, 60" x 58". Individually shaded blocks are stacked and surrounded with a watercolor background, giving the illusion of ascending fog.*

When viewed closely, the color and design elements of the individual squares do not look like they will blend together, but they do when viewed from afar.

Spend some time reading and rereading this section and looking at the photographs before you start working on the design wall. You'll begin to understand the basic techniques for getting started, see how to lay down a graded wash using fabric squares, and start to think in terms of value first, color second. You will grasp the importance of frequent evaluation in order to identify and solve problems. You will discover new ways to use individual squares and explore techniques on how to depict flowers, build bridges, and develop pockets that hold color. You will be increasingly challenged as you study and work on your project.

General Rules

- ❧ Above all, remember, rules can be broken!
- ❧ Do not use too many pieces of the same fabric, except for special effects.
- ❧ Do not place pieces from the same fabric in areas that are close together.
- ❧ Use only a few super darks and super lights.
- ❧ Think about value first and color second to produce a smoothly graded wash effect.

Getting Started

Beginning to work on the design wall is like approaching any project or solving any problem—there is almost always more than one method or solution. We each work in a different manner, and neither is better than the other. Choose one of the following methods that you think will work best for you, or use one of your own.

Pat's Method

Pat keeps both value and color in mind as she quickly picks up pieces and systematically produces a value run from light to dark (or dark to light). She finds it easier to think, "Go darker, go even darker, go even darker than that." The same holds true for going toward lighter values. She needs to work in a natural progression without jumping back and forth. She creates each shaded run of values, whether within a square or within

a bar, separately and completely before going on to a different area. She picks up pieces and tries them. If she feels the jump is too big between those already on the wall and the new one she is trying, she places the new one in the approximate position where it belongs. She compares each new fabric square to those already on the wall.

The beginning of Pat's project

Pat refers to her road map as she goes. Her finished size may not be the same as that indicated on the plan. However, this does not bother her if the flow of value is smooth and appealing.

At the same time she is thinking lighter or darker, Pat also considers color. Each new square contains some of the same color as its neighboring squares. For example, if she is working with squares that have a predominantly blue feeling and the next square she picks up not only suggests blue but also green, she may begin to work in greens or teals for a while. Somewhere along the way, she picks up a fabric square that suggests another color change. Not only does a smooth value change occur, but a wonderful color "run" or "smear" develops as well.

Donna's Method

Donna finds it easier to get started by thinking in terms of value only. Color is incidental to her process of creating a wash of color. She does not have a detailed sketch. Therefore, it takes her longer to get started because she builds a road map shortly after getting into the project. She spends a great deal of time visualizing the design. With a clear image and its shadings from light to dark in her mind, she is ready to begin. It is important to note that the finished quilt may not resemble this original image. The designs sometimes have a mind of their own and want to go their own way. Donna tries to be flexible and flow with the design process rather than fight it. This delightful spontaneity leads to new directions and encourages creativity.

Using the picture in her mind, she works quickly, placing twenty-five to thirty squares on the design wall in an area that starts light and gradually gets darker. She uses a box of fabrics sorted by value, not color. At this point, she is thinking about values and mood and creating an area that "feels" light, airy, and perhaps delicate. She places pale yellows, creams, pinks, blues, and greens next to each other quickly and spontaneously. The criterion for using a square is that its value and design lines must blend with the neighboring squares. After arranging these squares for a few minutes, she stands back to evaluate her progress with the reducing tool and a value finder. Looking for

an overall effect of blending and a light mood, she does not pay attention to individual squares unless they are blatantly wrong. Refining comes later.

If the squares on the design wall do not blend softly or if they do not agree with the image in her mind, she moves them. Again, she stands back often and uses the tools that help her evaluate the design.

When Donna is satisfied she is on the right track with these first few squares, she plans her strategy to interpret the entire design. Referring to the picture in her mind, she places six or seven light value squares in each of the light areas and does the same for the dark areas of the design. These squares serve as "markers" or guides. She might place a row of squares along the outer limits of the design to locate the edge of the quilt. Next, Donna stands back and evaluates the basic design by checking the

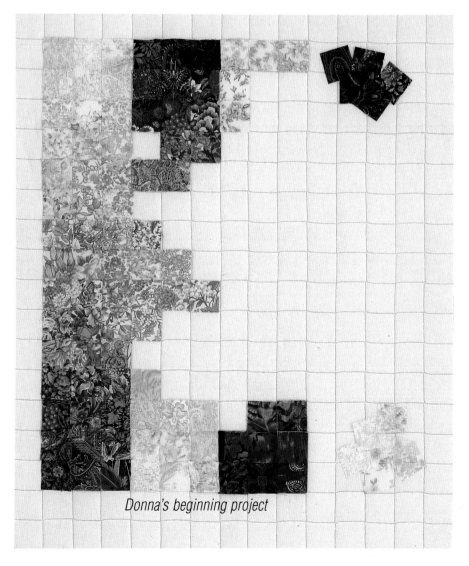

Donna's beginning project

balance, light source, lines, rhythm, motion, and overall effect. Sometimes she rearranges and adapts the markers until she is satisfied with the composition of the design. Sometimes she moves the markers to create different effects as the design progresses.

As Donna continues to work on the project, she works not only from light to dark but also finds it helpful to work from the dark area toward the lighter end of the graded wash. Working backward sets the limits by establishing the medium area where the two values must meet. Each square placed on the wall is a little lighter or darker than the neighboring squares to establish the subtle shading and to keep it flowing. "Mooshing" is our term for this melting and blending effect. Donna keeps her eye on the overall effect that is developing to avoid getting stuck in any one spot.

Runs of color develop spontaneously. When several squares together suggest a particular color family, Donna picks up the box that contains squares of this color and works with them, using value and color to achieve a "run" or "smear" effect.

As you practice and learn the watercolor and Impressionistic techniques in a fabric medium, you will gain self-confidence. For example, the third color run comes together easier and faster and looks better than the first two. Continue working, laying down washes, letting colors run and smear, developing accents and highlights. Continually evaluate and analyze the work as you progress.

Evaluating Your Work

Because it is difficult to keep your perspective when working in an absorbed manner close to the wall, it is important to occasionally turn your back on the design wall and walk at least ten feet away from it. Then turn around and squint at your work or use a reducing tool and value finder. They will help you visualize how the design will look after it is sewn together. Analyze the project. Diagnose and solve problem areas by asking yourself the following questions.

- Are the value changes subtle and gradual; is there a smooth flow where the fabrics blend and "moosh" together or does the eye stop at the edge of some of the squares?
- Do individual squares appear to jump out or look wrong? Are they out of value sequence? Are they too bright or too dull?
- Do the color runs harmonize with the balance of the design?
- Do squares "moosh" together to convey a feeling of texture or are there too many details?
- Are there hints of interest areas to develop later?

Based on your answers to these questions, rework the problem areas. Rotate the squares, flip them over, or relocate them. Try to think of fresh solutions. Eliminate unwanted lines or breaks that destroy the smooth value shadings you have created.

Look at your piece in bright light and dim light, daylight and artificial light. Occasionally, stand back and off to one side in order to look at the work from that angle, reducing the image so patterns of color, balance, rhythm, and motion become clear. Look at the reflection of the design in a mirror. Leave the room for a while. When you return, you will see the project with a fresh eye and notice some areas that look great and other places that don't satisfy you.

This is the time to remember that each square will have ¼"-wide seam allowance removed from each side. Try to disregard the colors and design elements at the outer edges of each piece. They will not contribute to your design because they are going to disappear forever under the presser foot of your sewing machine.

Be sure to evaluate yourself. Do you feel bogged down and discouraged? Do you hear heavy sighs even though you are the only one in the room? Perhaps it is time to pat the dog, play with the kitties, or even start supper. When you come back, you will see your design from a fresh perspective and new ideas will develop.

Sometimes you will catch yourself looking for the "perfect square." Stop! This type of concentration inhibits the flow of creativity. You become tired and frustrated. Go to the design wall and put new squares up or rearrange a few prints. Your eye will find that perfect fabric later when you are not even looking for it.

Using Individual Squares

Bridging Squares (to help you over troubled waters)

When you are looking for one square to fit in a special place, find a fabric that will serve as a bridge between the squares. It will be a square that has many values and colors to connect all the surrounding squares.

Back-Side Squares (for when you can't face the world and need help!)

The back side of a fabric is often the perfect choice for creating a softer, more muted look. If a print is too bright, flip it over. The back side is usually less intense.

Rotating Squares (or "Honey, see if I look better upside down!")

Due to the color, line, and/or value distribution within each square, you will sometimes find one that looks out of place. It may be more pleasing standing on its head or lying on its side, so try rotating squares. Try quarter-turns and half-turns before you decide to eliminate the offending square.

An uneven line is the result of value not flowing smoothly. Rework this area.

Perfect – reaches out.

Rotate ½ turn!

Turn over.

Good bridging square.

Too light

Watercolor graded wash before final tune-up

Perfect Squares (the "Goody-Two-Shoes" squares that do everything right)

Sometimes you need to cut out special motifs or parts of fabric designs to fit in special places. Perhaps you need a pink square with one purple corner—or one red petal or a diagonal line. Using a window template (page 21) or the Ruby Beholder, place it on the fabric and move it around until you find the square you need. The window template shows you how the square will look after cutting and sewing. Cut around the outside edge of this template, which includes the seam allowance.

You might have difficulty finding the perfect fabric with the perfect square. Check your fabric library. It really is OK to cut a 2" square out of the middle of a new piece of fabric. Of course, when all else fails, there's always the fabric store.

Developing Areas of Interest

"Mooshing"

This is our term for making the colors, values, and printed designs blend. When the design is viewed from a distance, the eye should flow along the piece without stopping on specific squares or edges.

Squares that "moosh" when seen from a distance (See "Tree of Heaven," page 74.)

There should be a feeling of texture without much detail, a subtle mood of graceful transition. Work with value and individual colors to carefully control the gradual blending. Lucy Kittrick's "Tree of Heaven," shown in the closeup below, left, is a wonderful example of "mooshing" fabrics and values to achieve a blending effect.

Making Background Floral Areas

To imitate an overall flower-garden feeling, choose medium-scale florals with similar values. Mass them together to give the illusion of fields of flowers. Use the wrong side of the fabric for a soft, diffused effect.

Individual fabrics used in a background floral area (See "Ribbon Serenade," page 73.)

These floral areas create moods and impressions rather than striking highlights. Donna's "Ribbon Serenade" on page 73 has floral areas that add to the flowing nature of her quilt. The close-up above shows the types of fabrics she used to create this effect. Make background floral areas interesting, but not so exciting that they take attention away from accents and highlights that develop. In the full-quilt photo, they have a lively, irregular quality with a feeling of texture but minimum detail. In other words, the fabrics in this area "moosh" together beautifully, and the transition between the squares is smooth and graceful.

Creating Pockets of Color

When working quickly to place the squares on the design wall, you may find several squares together often suggest an individual color. Capitalize on this by adding a few more squares, blending both value and color. Sometimes you only need to add a few squares to give the impression of a color. At other times, use more fabrics to expand the area. These effects can be light and airy or dark and rich. Make sure there is a soft diffusion and good flow between color pockets.

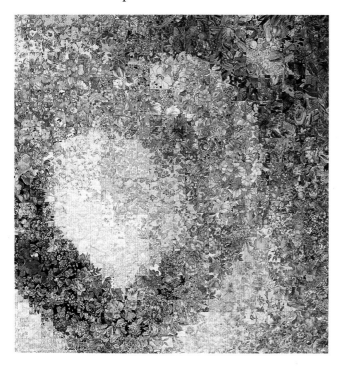

Fabrics grouped together to show pockets of color
(See page 72.)

In the "Heart's Delight" close-up shown above, Donna captured the soft pinks and blues of summer flowers and added yellows, golds, and rusts for unexpected contrast.

Running or Smearing Colors

Visualize the watercolorist adding water to the pigments, floating colors on the wet areas of the painting and watching them diffuse and run into other areas and colors. Refer to the watercolor paintings on page 33. Try to achieve similar effects with your fabrics. Place squares from one color family in an area. Experiment with

controlling this color to let it slowly diffuse and shift into another color or even into a background "wash" or floral area. The color should run effortlessly, as if the design wall has been tipped to cause the paint to travel in a new direction. Where the diffusion takes place, there is "mooshing" and blending that makes the transition between the colors soft and subtle.

A smear of color (See "Religious Theme III: Everlasting Promises," page 94.)

In the lower right-hand corner of "Religious Theme III: Everlasting Promises," shown in the close-up above, Donna allowed the blue-green to swirl and smear into other values and colors.

Recreating Flowers and Other Shapes

In watercolor quilts, floral shapes look complex yet realistic. Actually, these flowers are loose interpretations rather than beautifully detailed blossoms. They are fun to create, and we enjoy them more than garden flowers—

Pat used various fabrics to create flowers in an Impressionistic style for the Window Box quilt. The hand-quilting lines utilize the lines of the petals to make the blossoms stand out. (See Window Box, page 68.)

because there are no weeds! When you cut up large-scale prints, only parts of petals, leaves, and other fragmented images remain. You can use the colors and lines in these squares as building blocks. This re-creation of new images is a freeing experience.

Group several petals from similar-colored squares, using different fabrics. Sometimes it is necessary to include several squares from the same fabric. This creates new blossoms. Pat created the flowers in her "Window Box" quilt in this manner. In the close-up above, notice how these new images are not perfectly shaped images of real flowers. The lines do not always meet and the colors may not match, especially when viewed up close. You are an Impressionistic artist; your eye will blur these imperfections. Stand back often to analyze and evaluate your design.

Creating the Illusion of Curves and Diagonal Lines

You can create diagonal and curved lines within your design without piecing or using triangles. Find fabric squares that contain good contrast in value or color and create curved or diagonal lines within the squares. Use these to make flowing lines or sharp angles without piecing the squares.

The close-up of the flames in Donna's quilt "Religious Theme III: Everlasting Promises," shown at right, shows how individual squares with contrasting values can be used to create the illusion of curves with no extra piecing required.

Donna created the illusion of curving flames with no extra piecing. Red metallic thread highlights this area of the quilt. The long, graceful curved quilting lines suggest wind currents. Close random quilting follows the lines of the prints. (See "Religious Theme III: Everlasting Promises," page 94.)

Tuning It Up

Refine and rework the design, constantly evaluating it. Analyze problem areas and try fresh ideas. Develop interesting shapes and flowers when appropriate. Continue to refine your project over a period of several days, which gives you the opportunity to view it in different lighting conditions. Time away from the project also helps your perspective. Use your reducing tool and a value finder, such as the Ruby Beholder. Above all, trust your own good judgment and intuition.

By now, you have discovered that playing with watercolor squares is addictive. Once you get started on a project, you probably won't be able to leave it alone. Dinner will be late. (It's a good idea to have the take-out, fast-food phone numbers pinned to your design wall.) Laundry will stack up; the housecleaning will wait. However, you probably won't notice.

One of our students came home after work one day to find the squares in her design had supernatural powers. They had traded places in her evolving composition on the design wall. After several days of detective work, she discovered the culprit was not her cat or the wind. Her husband finally confessed that he was having as much fun as she was!

Even when family members and friends don't take an active role in the project, they definitely have an opinion on how the quilt is coming along and which squares don't fit. You may find their comments helpful, and they might enjoy expressing an opinion.

Young children often show an interest in the design process. Give them their own stack of squares. They love working with fabric designs such as animals, cars, and faces. They will learn a lot about color as they play.

You, too, will learn many things as you play with the squares. You will learn how to make color value and intensity work for you to achieve the effects you want. The time will finally come when you say to yourself, *"After midnight tonight, I will not move another square. Tomorrow, I will sew."*

Get a good night's sleep.

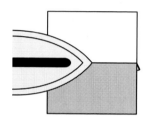

Today, I Sew

W̲e wish we could tell you a quick method for sewing your watercolor squares together. However, we are afraid there isn't one—no strip, cut, and resew for this project! Besides, that would take away from enjoying each and every print one more time.

You will be shocked to see the quilt top shrink before your eyes as you sew it together. Even though you are prepared, it is still pretty amazing. To avoid surprises, count the squares across and down and multiply by 1½" to discover the size your design will be after stitching.

FOUR RULES FOR WATERCOLOR QUILT TOP ASSEMBLY

Rule #1: Do not mix up the squares. Be careful to sew the squares together in the right order. This is not the time to try rotation! Place a pin in the first square of each row as a marker to help you remember where a new row begins.

Rule #2: Press carefully. Do not use steam until quilt top is completed. First, set the seams. Place the squares on the pressing board exactly as they were sewn, right sides together. Press the seam allowances flat, using a lifting, up-and-down motion with the iron. Do not *iron* the fabrics; it causes stretching and distortion.

After setting the seams, turn the squares to the right side and press the seam allowances to one side.

Sew the squares together in vertical or horizontal rows, then set the seam allowances as described above and press the seams to one side, alternating the direction from row to row. Pressing in this manner makes the seam allowances nestle together nicely for the next step.

To keep confusion to a minimum:
1. Press seams in the odd-numbered rows up.
2. Press seams in the even-numbered rows down.
   (It is easy to remember because odd and up are short words and belong together. Even and down are longer words with the same number of letters.)

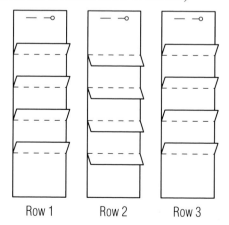

Row 1   Row 2   Row 3

Rule #3: After pressing the seam allowances in each row of squares as described on page 44, pin the rows together. When you place the rows right sides together for sewing, there will be a seam allowance on each side of the place where seam lines come together. These are "opposing seam allowances" because the seam allowances were pressed in opposite directions; they nestle together easily, and the bulk of the layers is distributed evenly at each seam intersection.

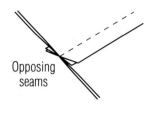

Opposing seams

To ensure precisely matched seams, *pin each intersection before sewing.* Stitch seams carefully so they are always straight with no gentle curves.

Rule #4: Sew row to row in opposing directions to avoid warping or curvature in the finished quilt top. If you always start sewing the rows together from the same edge of the quilt, the top for example, the finished quilt top may develop a warped appearance, and the whole piece will curve to one side. It will not be square when completed. To remedy this, you will need to alternate where you begin sewing the rows.

To remember where you started sewing each row, do the following:

When sewing Rows 1 and 2 together, leave long threads at the beginning of that seam. Clip the threads short where you finish the seam. When adding Row 3, start where you clipped the end threads short on Row 2. Continue alternating in this manner to complete the quilt top. (Arrows indicate stitching direction.)

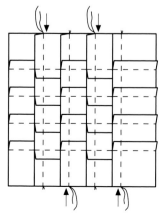

READY, SET, STITCH

There are four methods from which to choose. Try the one that appeals to you most. With each one, it is important to use an accurate ¼"-wide seam allowance. To make quicker work of the piecing, we recommend that you fill several bobbins with good-quality, 100% cotton, neutral-colored thread. Use the same thread in the top and bobbin.

Sew the squares together in either vertical or horizontal rows. The finished quilt top will subtly reflect the direction you chose, because when the rows are sewn together, ridges develop where seam allowances are pressed to one side. There will be a subtle vertical or horizontal look to the seams. Plan ahead and use this effect to enhance your piece.

Method 1—Slow but Sure

Probably the easiest and safest way to stitch the squares together is one row at a time. You are less apt to get mixed up if you are interrupted. Use a "bridge" between the squares as you sew them together to save time and thread. (See tip box on page 46.) Keep the rows in order by pinning them to the design wall when finished.

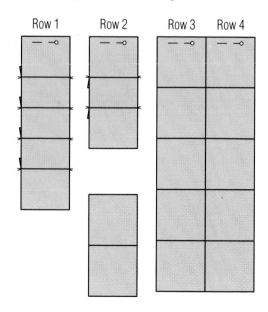

Follow directions given earlier in this chapter for pressing and sewing the rows together.

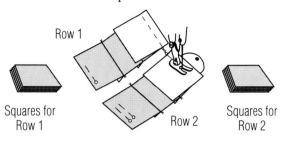

Using a Bridge

If you are tired of clipping long threads when sewing projects, try our gizmo, called a *bridge*. To make a bridge, place two rectangles of fabric together (each approximately ¾" x 2"). When it is time to remove the sewn squares from the machine, do not lift the presser foot or clip threads. Instead, run the bridge through the machine; clip the sewn squares off the back. When you are ready to begin sewing, ease new squares under the presser foot without lifting it. Cut the bridge off the back. This technique saves time and thread.

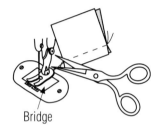

Bridge

Method 2—A Little Faster, but It Takes Concentration

This method uses the "chain piecing" technique to sew two rows at the same time and speed things along. The disadvantage is that it is easy to get the squares mixed up if you don't concentrate. This method saves time as well as thread. See pages 96–97 for instructions on how to chain piece.

1. Carefully remove a row of squares from the design wall and stack them in the correct order to the left of the sewing machine. This is Row 1. Place one pin in the first square to mark where you started.
2. Remove and stack a second row of squares and place them in the correct order to the right of the machine. Place two pins in the first square, marking this as Row 2.
3. Sew the first two squares of Row 1 together, then the first two squares of Row 2, using the chaining technique.

4. Continue adding new squares to the end of each row that does not have pins in it.

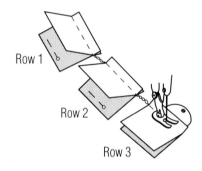

Row 1

Squares for Row 1

Row 2

Squares for Row 2

Follow directions given earlier for pressing and sewing the rows together.

If you feel brave, you can use this method to sew more than two rows at one time.

Method 3—The Squares Stay Connected

This technique also involves chaining the squares.

1. Place a pin in the top square of each vertical row, marking them as the "top" of the quilt. Chain the first two squares of each row through the machine.

Row 1

Row 2

Row 3

2. After sewing the final two squares, remove the chain of squares from the machine, but do not cut them apart. Because each top square was marked with a pin, it is easy to see where the top of the row is, even if the squares twirl. Add the third square to the bottom of each row, again chaining.

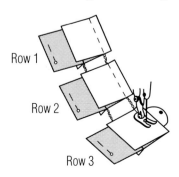

Row 1

Row 2

Row 3

Do not cut them apart. Continue adding squares, chaining but not clipping threads, until the entire piece is finished. Clip the threads.

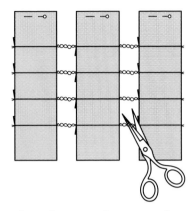

Press and sew the vertical rows together, as described earlier, in order to complete the quilt top.

Method 4—Blocks Instead of Rows

This method seems complicated, but the only tricky part is being careful to pay attention when pressing seam allowances. Sew the squares together in blocks of sixteen, then sew the blocks together. This helps eliminate the warping and curving lines that can occur when sewing many long rows of squares together.

1. Remove the top four squares of Row 1 from the design wall and place them in the same order on the left side of your sewing machine. Do the same with the first four squares of Rows 2, 3, and 4. Place one pin in the first square of Row 1, two pins in the first square of Row 2, three pins in the first square of Row 3, and four pins in the first square of Row 4.

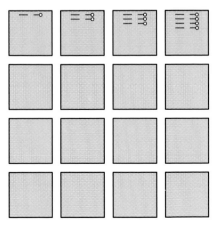

2. Sew the squares together to make rows. Set the seams and press the seam allowances, using the following sequence for each block of squares:
Row 1 and Row 3: Press seams up.
Row 2 and Row 4: Press seams down.

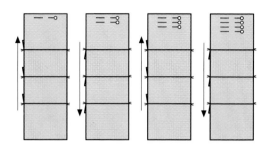

3. Place Row 1 and Row 2 right sides together. Pin carefully at the opposing seam allowances and sew these rows together. Add Row 3 and Row 4. Do not press these seam allowances yet.

4. Continue making blocks and pin them to the design wall to keep them in the correct order.

5. Sew the blocks together in rows, but first set and press the three vertical seam allowances in each block in the following manner. Press the seam allowances in the odd-numbered blocks to the left. Press the seam allowances in the even-numbered blocks to the right.

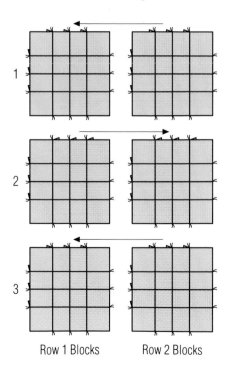

Row 1 Blocks   Row 2 Blocks

Alternating the direction of the pressed seam allowances ensures that seam intersections come together precisely and the seam allowances are evenly distributed so they nestle together for precisely matched seams.

6. After sewing the blocks into rows, press the seams joining the blocks so that seams are in opposing directions (up for odd-numbered rows and down for even-numbered rows).

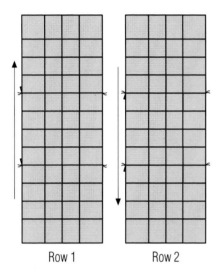

Row 1   Row 2

Pin carefully. Sew the rows of blocks together by beginning each seam at opposite ends as described on page 45.

DON'T BE PRESSED FOR TIME

Press the entire top, using steam, so all seams lie flat. Pin the top to the design wall and look at it from a short distance. Don't panic! Remember, we said the piece would shrink while sewing. Do not evaluate the project at this time—it is too late to rearrange the squares.

Congratulate yourself and pat yourself on the back. Maybe now you will have time to finish that delicious chocolate mousse!

OTHER JOURNEYS— PLANNING YOUR NEXT ONE

You can expand on any idea to create your next watercolor design. After your first watercolor success, the next one will be easier, and you'll see more and do more along the way. Get the maps ready—let's go.

Other Shapes

Sometimes it is impossible to produce a diagonal line in a design without using a triangle. When you are faced with this problem, do not make a template and cut more fabric. Use the method described on page 97, instead. Karen Pederson used half-square triangles in "Stained Glass Garden" on page 95 to create beautifully shaded octagons, using value rather than color. "Liberty Star" by Kathleen Butts, pictured on page 80, effectively explores the use of squares and triangles. The images give one a feeling of pattern and light. Thine Bloxham achieved a unique effect in her "Woven Ribbon" quilt on page 91 by using only triangles.

In addition to using squares and squares made from triangles, you can try the same process, using different geometric shapes—triangles, rectangles, hexagons, trapezoids, or diamonds.

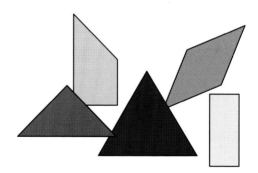

Keep in mind that it is necessary to cut more fabric when using any one of these other shapes. Pat used a modified trapezoid shape in "Braidings," pictured on page 58, to achieve elegant, shaded rows of braids. Notice how one row goes from dark to light, the next row from light to dark, and so on.

Traditional Patchwork Patterns

Adapting a traditional block pattern for use in a watercolor quilt is challenging and exciting. Anne Morton used various star block patterns in "Blue Star Galaxy" on page 83. She placed the stars on a shaded background that contains wonderful pockets of color to create space and movement. Ree Nancarrow also used several star block patterns in "Galaxy" on page 83. The half-stars in the border provide a rich finish to the overall impression of the design.

Other Techniques

What about combining watercolor-quilt methods with other techniques, such as appliqué or broderie perse? The combination of straight-line piecing and curved-line motifs enhance each other. Remember to keep it simple. The beauty of watercolor quilts and the effect they have on the viewer lies in their simple, yet complex, nature. Techniques or designs that are too elaborate can detract from the overall composition of the piece and make it look too busy.

In her quilt "It's Better Down Under" on page 84, Shirley Perryman successfully combined watercolor-quilt techniques with appliqué. She designed the background first to create impressions of water and light. Then she appliquéd the underwater motifs to produce an exotic and intriguing design.

Karla Harris's quilt on page 87 features a moose made from 1" squares. She used long strips of light-colored fabric to create the background area of the center circle. By placing this design on a watercolor background and adding appliquéd leaves and flowers, Karla masterfully created an original design that combines contemporary and traditional techniques. "beyond Alces" started as a small mock-up and grew from there.

"Silver Lattice" by Margaret K. Fortune on page 92 features the broderie perse technique, which adds a particularly graceful feeling to the design. The curving lines of the flowers soften and complement the watercolor background.

Inspiration

Cross-stitch and needlepoint designs serve as another source of inspiration. They are formulated in a multisquare format that makes it easy to adapt to watercolor quilt designs. To adapt a design of this type to watercolor quilting:

1. Choose a simple motif that allows for shading within the motif as well as in the background.
2. Draw the motif on graph paper.
3. Overlay the basic design with a sheet of tracing paper. Have fun shading to your heart's content until the perfect design emerges. Pat designed "Homespun Heartstrings," shown on page 70, in this manner. A cross-stitch pattern was the inspiration for "My House Calls" by Janie Perino, shown on page 75. The shading for this quilt appears on page 32.

Potential quilt designs may also come from photos, greeting cards, gift wrap, and pictures. A greeting card featuring floral motifs was the inspiration for Donna's "Heart's Delight," shown on page 72.

A personal moment in time—experiencing an especially beautiful sunrise or a spectacular waterfall, or walking through a special flower garden—may be the ultimate inspiration for your next watercolor quilt. If such an experience presents itself, take a photograph or make a sketch with notes about value and color changes and any other elements of the scene you would like to capture in your design. Then go home and make a shaded plan on graph paper that will lead to a quilt.

FRAME IT!

Once your design is pieced, hang it on a wall where you can see it frequently over a period of several days. Observe it in both natural and artificial light. As you reflect on ideas for borders, backing fabrics, and quilting lines, make mental or written notes that capture the suggestions which enhance the theme of your design.

Most pieces of art need a frame to contain and stop the flow of the design. Just as a beautiful work of art is enhanced by its frame, watercolor quilts need carefully selected fabric borders. When framing an original Monet painting, you would not choose a black aluminum poster frame. Your quilt is also an original piece of art, so give border selection the same careful consideration you gave to the design of the pieced top.

To get started, study the borders on the quilts pictured in this book. Notice that most of them are simple and uncomplicated. They do not overpower the design. Some of the quilts have a narrow, inner border, similar to a mat in a watercolor painting. If you choose to add this feature to help draw the eye to the beauty of the piece, select a fabric that complements the design. Some examples of quilts with inner borders are "Stained Glass Garden" by Karen Pederson on page 95, "Grizzly" by Ree Nancarrow on page 87, and "beyond Alces" by Karla Harris on page 87. The inner border of Donna's "Dawn's Early Light" on page 66 features her husband Lloyd's hand-painted fabric.

Occasionally, the design will have a visually built-in border. In Donna's "My Morning Garden" on page 73, the dark outer edge suggests a border, and the binding serves as a narrow frame. Other projects need a border to feel

A Fine Finish

complete. When selecting fabric to use as a frame, consider color as well as the width of the border. A dark print that has the appearance of a solid color from a distance works nicely. It gives an impression of subtle texture and brings out the gentle glowing effect of luminosity in the quilt.

The process of selecting a frame for your work is what we call a "comparison test." It is similar to a multiple-choice question on an exam, where there is one right answer, several that are almost correct, and some that are obviously wrong. You read and compare all the choices to see which answer best fits the question. You do the same with bolts of fabric (possible answers) and the pieced watercolor design (the question).

To select a border for your watercolor composition, visit your quilt shop with your quilt top in hand. If you ask, most shops will let you lay it out on a table or on the floor in a quiet corner. Select several bolts of fabric that might be good choices for framing your project. Unroll at least a yard of fabric from bolt #1. Place the project on top of this fabric so that several inches of the fabric imitate a border around one corner of the quilt top.

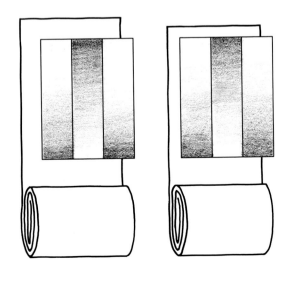

Check this possible "answer" against the "question." Does this color bring out the best in your design? Using the same procedure, try bolt #2. Which of these fabrics looks better? Eliminate the one you like the least. Try several more bolts, always comparing new fabrics with the best choice thus far.

As you contemplate color choices, take note of the border width. Change the amount of exposed border fabric; try various widths from very narrow to very wide. Which width enhances your design best? If you have an inner border, use the same method to analyze it with both the watercolor piece and the outer border. All factors need to work in harmony.

When you are down to the final few possibilities, be sure the border fabric looks good against all four sides. By now, you probably have enough quilters helping you to hold a quilt-guild meeting! Listen to their advice as you may discover new ideas, but remember that *you* need to make the final choice. After all, you will have to live with it. (Be sure to ask your advisors to help you carry all those bolts back to the shelves!)

Apply the borders with either straight-cut or mitered corners. It is your choice. For additional information on applying borders, see pages 99–101.

BACK IT!

There is much more to a quilt than what you see on the front. Quilters are well aware of the temptation to pick up the edge of a quilt to look at the back side. The back gives you another opportunity to make a statement. Today, many quilts are reversible—back art is very popular.

When planning the back treatment, keep the total design of the front in mind. It is an adventure to select a fabric for the back of the quilt that coordinates with the front. Pick out themes, motifs, colors, and textures used in the design and let them be your inspiration.

You might want to consider a pieced backing that reflects an idea suggested by the themes on the front of the quilt. Sharon Wiser found a wonderful novelty print to combine with an appliquéd skyline for the back of her quilt "Urban Dawn," pictured on page 76. This backing expresses the same theme as the front of the quilt as well as adding a whimsical touch of humor.

A backing that reflects the theme of the quilt design. (See "Urban Dawn," page 76.)

Stagger seams in the backing with those on the front whenever possible for minimal bulk as shown in the illustration below.

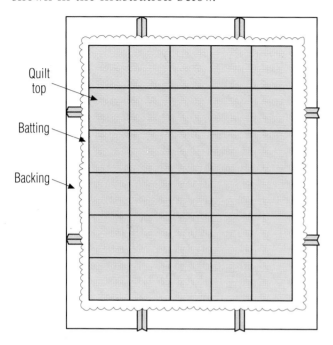

Quilt top

Batting

Backing

On the front of a watercolor quilt, seam allowances are 1½" apart. For hand quilters, this already means difficult needling. You will probably want to keep back piecing to a minimum. For machine quilters, of course, the sky is the limit.

Pat likes to choose a fabric that has the same dominant colors and mood as the front. Since she is a hand quilter, she does not piece her backings any more than necessary.

Because she is a machine quilter, Donna often pieces her quilt backings. The mood and colors are very different on the front and back, but the quilt is united by the theme.

For additional information on backing your quilt, see page 101.

QUILT IT!

In art, we often consider three-dimensional pieces as sculptures. It is difficult to call quilts a form of sculpture, and yet they definitely have surface relief produced by the quilting stitches. The watercolor quilt has a typically more contemporary look than a traditional quilt. It is full of moods and emotions. Lighting effects, produced by blending values rather than using patterns, provide contrast. The design has depth and moves the eye. Watercolor quilts are, by nature, definitely not flat and static. Therefore, select a quilting design that can be integrated with the design of the pieced top so that the mood, special effects, and feeling of the piece are all enhanced by the quilting design.

Up to this point, in creating your watercolor quilt top, you worked entirely with squares and other straight-line geometric shapes. You made lines, colors, and values flow from square to square in order to de-emphasize these straight lines and to help the eye blur the "daubs" into a unified composition. Your quilting lines should do the same in order to complement your work.

Nontraditional, fluid, curved lines help camouflage and break up the many seams. Traditional quilting lines, stitched ¼" away from the seams, will only chop up the design and emphasize the edges of the squares that you spent hours trying to hide and blend. Free-form swirls bring out moods. Swooping lines suggest movement and force the eyes to follow them across the quilt. Use curved lines in combination with straight lines to create special effects. In "Lifting Fog," Pat used swirling quilting lines in simple curves that move across the quilt surface, softening the angles and straight lines, and giving the design an impression of gentle motion.

Pat's loose and flowing hand-quilting lines depict the feeling and motion of swirling fog. See "Lifting Fog," page 35.)

To become familiar with nontraditional quilting lines, practice doodling swirls and curved lines on paper (perhaps while talking on the telephone to another quilter about next month's quilt show). Nature and even ordinary objects take on new meaning when looking for quilting designs. Gentle rolling hills, graceful arching tree branches, the tail of a kite caught by the wind, the curve of a lamp, or a rocking chair—all of these can serve as inspiration for quilting lines.

Lay a piece of tracing paper over your original drawing of the quilt design. Sketch a quilting design on this paper. Try several designs until you find the one you feel best complements your watercolor design. Yumiko Hirasawa used this technique for her "Goraiko"— Rising Sun quilt. (See page 85.)

You can emphasize some areas by using stipple or echo quilting techniques to create special effects. Donna often uses "random" quilting lines, her favorite technique for filling in areas. Similar to stipple quilting, random quilting lines allow you to stitch over previous stitching while following outlines and shapes in the piece. An example of random quilting lines is pictured in the closeup photograph of "Religious Theme III: Everlasting Promises" on page 42.

Remember, close quilting flattens areas but gives a feeling of texture. More open quilting lines allow the batting loft to expand, giving more obvious high and low areas of relief to the surface.

Some quilters like to use novelty threads, such as rayon or metallic, to highlight areas of their design with quilting stitches. The flames in "Religious Theme III: Everlasting Promises" on page 42 are subtly highlighted with red metallic thread.

Donna quilts small memory characters in each quilt. There are hearts for family members, a treble clef and notes to show the importance of music in her life, and her husband's name is hidden in every quilt. Several motifs reflect events that happened as she worked on a particular project. Her finished quilts are like puzzles with hidden mementos of her life.

Pat is a hand quilter who enjoys doing close, random quilting, particularly in the areas of her quilts that suggest a foggy or misty feeling. She chooses ripples for water, air motion in her sky, and rolling lines that suggest topographical irregularities. Sometimes she extends these lines out into the borders, as in "Lifting Fog" on page 35.

Impressionistic flowers or other images may be enhanced by quilting around their edges or along lines of details, such as petals. These lines pull all the individual colors and lines together to give the relief needed to make these images and flowers more realistic. Pat's "Window Box," shown in the close-up on page 42, provides an example of this type of quilting.

Quilting designs bring life to the pieced top design. Stretch your imagination. Allow yourself to be free.

SIGN IT! *(before the memories fade)*

If you want to give your quilts the credibility of an art form, you need to sign your work, just as artists do. Donna prefers to quilt her name in the lower right-hand corner of the quilt in addition to placing a label on the back of the quilt. Pat enjoys making a fancy label to appliqué on the back of the quilt. We both write pertinent information in permanent ink on the back of the quilt under the label. See page 109 for information on making labels.

We became aware of the importance of labels when Pat had a quilt top stolen in the summer of 1991. It was not signed. This quilt is now anonymous. We don't like the sound of that word. We don't want our quilts to be anonymous.

With all the quilt registration programs now in existence, quilts with documentation receive special attention. Much of our country's quilt history has been lost because quilters didn't take time to add their signatures to their quilts. Perhaps they did not feel their work was deserving of a signature.

We hope you will sign all of your quilts. Generations from now, your family will thank you. Do this favor for them today.

> "Every experience deeply felt in life needs to be passed along—whether it be through words and music, chiseled in stone, painted with a brush, or sewn with a needle, it is a way of reaching for immortality."
>
> ~ THOMAS JEFFERSON

The broderie perse appliqué on the label mirrors the design on the front of Margaret Fortune's quilt, "Silver Lattice," shown on page 92.

Pat made this beautiful label, depicting the feeling of "Lifting Fog," page 35.

SHOW IT OFF!

To get the full impact of watercolor quilts, you should hang them where they can be seen often. The special effects in a watercolor quilt take on different characteristics when viewed in different lighting conditions. Plan to enjoy the changing nature of these effects.

To make a sleeve for your quilt for easy hanging, see page 108. Select a fabric that complements the quilt and the backing. The backing fabric is a good choice for an inconspicuous sleeve.

Consider installing track lighting to spotlight your masterpiece. And while you're at it, purchase a plant pedestal to locate nearby, and add an arrangement of fresh flowers from your garden—or treat yourself and call your favorite florist. You deserve it!

The journey is over, so—

    Send out the invitations.
    Sit down.
    Relax.
    Break out the champagne.
    It's Show Time!

Watercolor Quilt Plans

The projects in this book are fairly simple and are excellent choices for a first watercolor quilt. The first quilt, "Braidings," is made of cutoff trapezoids instead of squares. Three of the projects begin with a watercolor design that serves as a background for appliqué or pieced designs. The watercolor backgrounds are attractive by themselves, so if you prefer, omit the appliqué or extra piecing for a very simple first quilt.

The directions for the individual projects are brief since each quilt will be a unique design based on the fabrics you choose. For additional guidance, study the photos and refer to information in other sections of this book as you work.

Read the Basic Quilt-making Techniques, beginning on page 96, for information on general quilt construction and basic finishing methods. It covers a wide variety of subjects, from how to sew accurate ¼"-wide seam allowances to adding the finishing touch—a quilt label—to your quilt. Sometimes there are two different instructions for accomplishing the same task; these reflect our individual way of doing things. We hope this section is informative in areas where you need help and that you pick up a new tip or two along the way.

Braidings

Finished Size: 26" x 25"

Braidings *by Patricia Maixner Magaret, 1990, Pullman, Washington, 26" x 25". A modified trapezoid shape is used to create subtle shaded areas in the bars.*

This charming quilt is an example of using a different geometric shape in place of the square to create a watercolor quilt. The pieces are arranged in rows of braids. In the traditional braid quilt, one side of the braid is light and the other side is dark. In the watercolor braid, each row goes from light to dark.

Materials: 44"-wide fabric

1 strip, 2"-wide, of each of approximately 60 different fabrics, in a wide range of values (You may use assorted scraps.)

⅞ yd. for border
½ yd. for binding
1 yd. for backing
batting

Cutting

Use template below.

1. Fold each 2"-wide strip in half with wrong sides together. Cut the trapezoid shape through both thicknesses. You will have only one T (Trapezoid) and only one Tr (Trapezoid reversed) from each fabric. Save the rest of the strip for future watercolor projects.

2. Cut 4 strips, each 3¼" wide, for the borders, cutting along the lengthwise grain.

Directions

1. Sort the T shapes by value. Sort the Tr shapes, using the same method. Keep the T shapes separate from the Tr shapes.

2. To create this design, you will use an odd-row configuration and an even-row configuration. On the design wall, build Row 1 (odd-row configuration), going from light to dark. Use approximately 20 trapezoids. You can adjust the length of the row to your liking by adding more or fewer of the pieces. Place the T shapes on the left-hand side of the braid and the Tr shapes on the right-hand side.

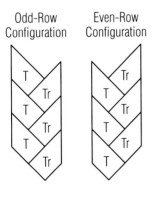

Odd-Row Configuration   Even-Row Configuration

3. Build Row 2 (even-row configuration). This time, go from dark to light. Build four more rows, reversing the value flow in each.

4. Begin sewing at the top of each braid. Sew the first two trapezoids as shown. Add the third piece and continue adding pieces down the braid.

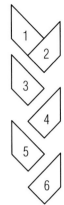

5. Join the braided rows and trim off points at the top and bottom edges.

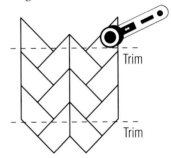

6. Attach borders, following the directions on pages 99–101.

7. Layer the completed quilt top with batting and backing; baste.

8. Quilt as desired.

9. Bind the edges. Sign and label your quilt.

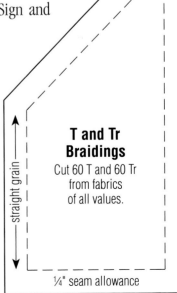

T and Tr Braidings
Cut 60 T and 60 Tr from fabrics of all values.

straight grain

¼" seam allowance

Lattice Rejoice!

Finished Size: 45" x 45"

Lattice Rejoice! *by Donna Ingram Slusser, assisted by Kirstin Martinson, 1993, Pullman, Washington, 45" x 45". A sunlit summer garden glows as one peeks through the floral-covered lattice. (Collection of Kirstin Martinson)*

The impression of looking through a lattice or trellis makes this quilt intriguing. The subtle shading of the summer garden is highlighted by a luminous effect that casts a sunlike glow over the design.

Materials: 44"-wide fabric

160 squares, each 2" x 2", in dark-medium to dark
    values for the lattice
376 squares, each 2" x 2", in light to medium values
    for garden background
1⅓ yds. for inner border
1⅓ yds. for outer border
½ yd. for binding
1½ yds. for backing
batting

Directions

Squares are set on the diagonal or "on point" in the finished quilt. Therefore, you must place them on point when you are working with them on the design wall. Take care to always align the points of the squares with the lines of the grid, whenever possible, to keep the design from going askew.

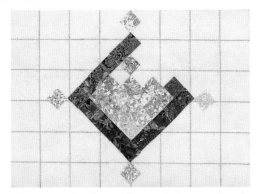

1. Referring to the design layout below and to the quilt photo, create the lattice first. Use dark-medium and dark squares. Working primarily with value, let a few impressions of color develop.

2. Build the background watercolor effect by keeping the lightest values in the upper right-hand corner, working gradually toward medium values in the center and the other three corners. These darker areas give the illusion of shadows or shade. Spontaneously create background floral areas or impressions of blossoms.

3. Sew the squares together, using Method 1 or Method 2 on pages 45–46. When you complete an individual row, pin it to the wall to keep the rows in the correct order.

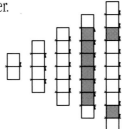

4. Sew the rows together. Trim off the points along the edges, leaving a ¼"-wide seam allowance all around.

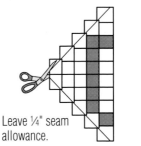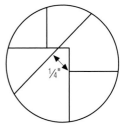

Leave ¼" seam
allowance.

5. Cut 4 strips, each 2" wide, for the inner border, cutting along the lengthwise grain.

6. For the outer border, cut 4 strips, each 5" x 48", cutting along the lengthwise grain of the fabric.

7. Sew each inner border strip to an outer border strip, matching center points. These 2 strips will now be treated as 1 border.

8. Attach the border to the quilt top, following the directions on pages 100–101 for adding borders with mitered corners.

9. Layer the quilt top with batting and backing; baste.

10. Quilt as desired.

11. Bind the edges. Sign and label your quilt.

Welcome

Finished Size: 12" x 29"

Welcome *by Karla Harris, 1992, Hope, Idaho,*
12" x 29". Combining watercolor techniques with
simple appliqué makes a charming addition to any
decor. Pieced and quilted by Wynona Harris King.

Watercolor and appliqué can be combined to create many unique designs. This project, though simply made, allows quiltmakers to express themselves by making a banner that will be appreciated by any guest.

Materials: 44"-wide fabric

96 assorted squares, each 2" x 2" (various colors in a
    wide range of values)
¼ yd. for "welcome" background
¼ yd. for appliqué letters
¼ yd. for binding
½ yd. for backing
batting

Directions

Use templates on the pullout pattern insert.
1. From the fabric for the welcome background, cut a
   panel 6½" x 24½".
2. Make templates for and cut each appliqué letter
   from the chosen fabric, following the directions on
   pages 97–98.
3. Appliqué the letters in place, referring to pages 97–
   99 for basic appliqué directions.
4. Design a watercolor border, following the diagram
   below for placement of the squares. As you work on
   the wall, the dimensions of the inner row of squares
   will be larger than the completed center panel because the 2" squares are the unfinished size. If you
   wish to double-check for accuracy, multiply the
   number of inside border squares times 1½" and add
   another ½" for seam allowances.

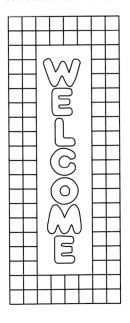

Choose a different color family for each border
corner. Then place the darkest square of each color
family in a corner and work toward the center with
lighter and lighter values. Refer to the quilt photo.
5. Sew the squares together to create 2 side border
   strips, each 2 squares across and 16 squares high.
   Sew the side borders to the center panel.
6. Sew the remaining squares together to create a top
   and bottom border, each 8 squares across and 2
   squares high. Sew to the top and bottom edges of the
   quilt top.
7. Layer the quilt top with batting and backing; baste.
8. Quilt as desired.
9. Bind the edges. Sign and label your quilt.

Hold Your Heads Up High

Finished Size: 35" x 36"

Hold Your Heads Up High *by Patricia Maixner Magaret, 1993, Pullman, Washington, 35" x 36". Tulips appliquéd on a watercolor background give the impression of a bright splash of spring color. A gift to Frank and Betty Maixner on the occasion of their fiftieth wedding anniversary.*

Watercolor backgrounds create a wonderful setting for appliqué designs. Any shading will work well. However, it appears more natural and pleasing if the majority of the dark area is placed at the bottom. The appliqué motifs that you want to highlight may look best if placed on a light, glowing area that gradually dims toward the edges, creating a medallion or cameo effect.

Materials: 44"-wide fabric

342 assorted squares, each 2" x 2" (various colors in a wide range of values)
small amounts of fabric or scraps for appliquéd flowers
1 yd. for inner border
1⅛ yds. for outer border
½ yd. for binding
1¼ yds. for backing
batting

Directions

Use templates on pullout pattern insert.

1. On your design wall, build a watercolor background, 18 squares wide and 19 squares long, or any size desired that will accommodate the appliqué design of your choice.
2. Sew the squares together.
3. Make templates for and cut each appliqué flower and leaf piece from the chosen fabric, following the directions on pages 97–98. Make bias stems.
4. Appliqué the tulips, stems, and leaves in place, referring to the basic appliqué directions on pages 97–99. The numbers on the appliqué pattern pieces refer to the order of appliqué.
5. From the inner border fabric, cut 4 strips, each 1¼" wide, cutting along the lengthwise grain.
6. From the outer border fabric, cut 4 strips, each 3¼" wide, cutting along the lengthwise grain.
7. Sew each inner border strip to an outer border strip, matching center points. These 2 strips will now be treated as 1 border.
8. Attach the border to the quilt top, following the directions for adding borders with mitered corners on pages 100–101.
9. Layer the quilt top with batting and backing; baste.
10. Quilt as desired.
11. Bind the edges. Sign and label your quilt.

Dawn's Early Light

Finished Size: 42" x 42"

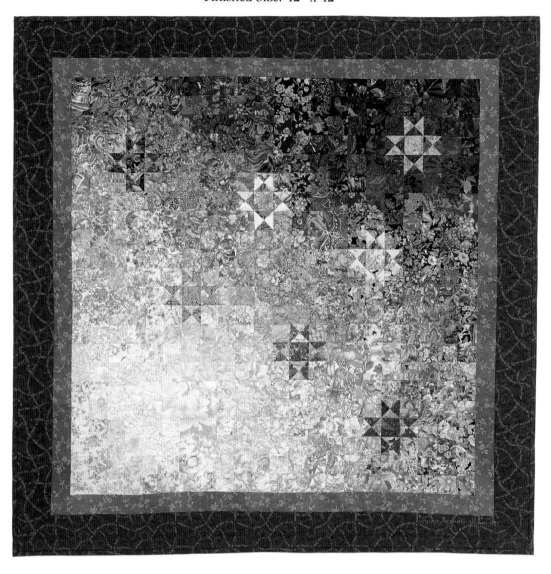

Dawn's Early Light *by Donna Ingram Slusser, 1993, Pullman, Washington, 42" x 42". Capturing the feeling of a beautiful early sunrise as stars slowly begin to disappear, Donna was inspired by the view from her hilltop home. A gift to her husband, Lloyd.*

The subtle watercolor background in this quilt gives an impression of early morning light—a backdrop for the Variable Star blocks that seem to float across the quilt surface. Some of the star fabrics almost blend with the background values, making them appear distant and mysterious.

Materials: 44"-wide fabric

484 squares, each 2" x 2", in a wide range of colors and values

1⅛ yds. for inner border

1⅓ yds. for outer border

½ yd. for binding

1½ yds. for backing

batting

Directions

1. On your design wall, build a watercolor background 22 squares wide by 22 squares long. Keep the lighter values near the bottom to create the glow of the hidden sun just below the line of the horizon. Gradually work toward the darker values of the night sky at the top of the design.

2. Make the pieced stars, using 2" squares pieced from quarter-square triangles. Study the placement and values of the stars in the photograph on page 66. Notice that some are lighter and brighter than others. Keeping values in mind, select fabrics for your stars. Fold the 2" squares for the star points in quarters diagonally and pin over the background squares as you design.

   a. Use some of your already-cut 2" fabric squares to cut and piece the star points, each of which consists of 4 quarter-square triangles. To make each star block, you will need 9 matching fabric squares, each 2" x 2", for the star points and the star center. For the background triangles, find squares that duplicate the fabric squares already on the wall where you plan to substitute the pieced stars. You will need:

   2 squares of the same background fabric for the left star points

   2 squares of the same background fabric for the right star points

   2 squares of the same background fabric for the top star points

   2 squares of the same background fabric for the bottom star points

   b. Make one pieced square at a time, using the template at right to cut 1 triangle from 2 squares of star fabric. Then cut 2 triangles from 1 set of background fabric squares.

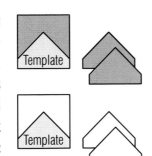

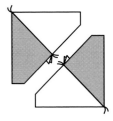

   c. Sew these 4 triangles together to make a pieced 2" square.

   d. Return this square to its correct place on the design wall before removing any other fabric squares. Make 3 more pieced 2" squares for the star points for this particular star. Note that there are 4 different background fabrics. Be sure to place the squares back on the design wall in the correct order after they are sewn. Place the remaining square of star fabric in the center of the star.

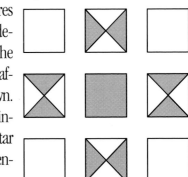

   e. Continue making star points until you have completed the desired number of stars and have positioned them on the design wall in the watercolor background design.

3. Sew the squares together to complete the quilt top.

4. From the inner border fabric, cut 4 strips, each 2" wide, cutting along the lengthwise grain.

5. From the outer border fabric, cut 4 strips, each 4½" wide, cutting along the lengthwise grain.

6. Sew each inner border strip to an outer border strip, matching center points. These 2 strips will now be treated as 1 border.

7. Attach the border to the quilt top, following the directions for adding borders with mitered corners on pages 100–101.

8. Layer the quilt top with batting and backing; baste.

9. Quilt as desired.

10. Bind the edges. Sign and label your quilt.

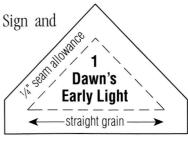

Window Box

Finished Size: 27½" x 32"

Window Box *by Patricia Maixner Magaret, 1992, Pullman, Washington, 27½" x 32". Pat re-created blossoms to produce a floral effect against a watercolor-graded wash. (Collection of Marilyn Bafus)*

Pat's charming quilt is easy to duplicate and provides practice in evaluating pieces for print scale as well as value. Use your window template to take full advantage of the large floral prints when cutting the 2" squares for the bottom portion of the design. Notice how the blossoms break into the side borders at the bottom of the quilt and continue to the outer edges, creating a window box effect.

Materials: 44"-wide fabric

252 squares, each 2" x 2", in a wide range of values and colors
90 squares (approximately), each 2" x 2", that contain parts of floral petals on a medium dark or dark background.
You may need additional squares as your design develops.
1 yd. dark print for border
½ yd. for binding
1 yd. for backing
batting

Directions

1. Referring to the quilt photo and working on your design wall, build the watercolor design, making it 14 squares wide and 18 squares long. Begin by creating a spotlight effect. Place the lightest value squares in the upper central portion of the design. Work out toward the two top corners and outer edges, using squares that are gradually darker (but still light) in value.
2. As you work down the quilt design, arrange squares in values that go from light to light darks. Create a pocket of warm color approximately in the center of the design.

3. Near the bottom of the quilt, create flowers by finding squares that contain individual petals on dark backgrounds. Refer to "Recreating Flowers and Other Shapes" on pages 41–42 for more information. Allow the flowers to extend 2 squares wide into each side border in the bottom 7 rows.
4. Disregarding the squares that are in the border, sew the remaining squares together, using your choice of the methods that begin on page 45.
5. From the border fabric, cut 2 strips along the lengthwise grain of fabric, each 3½" x 17", for the side borders. Piece the 2" squares in each side border and attach to the bottom of the side borders.

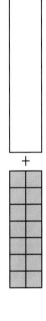

6. Attach the side borders, matching the bottom 7 rows of squares to those in the quilt top so the flower box extends all the way across the bottom of the quilt.
7. From the border fabric, cut 2 strips along the lengthwise grain of fabric. Cut 1 strip, 3½" x 27½", for the top border and 1 strip, 2" x 27½", for the bottom border. Attach the top and bottom borders.
8. Layer the quilt top with batting and backing; baste.
9. Quilt as desired.
10. Bind the edges. Sign and label your quilt.

Gallery of Quilts

Homespun Heartstrings *by Patricia Maixner Magaret, 1993, Pullman, Washington, 64" x 54". Inspired by a cross-stitch design, Pat used heart motifs to represent each member of her family.*

Morning Glory *by Patricia Maixner Magaret, 1992, Pullman, Washington, 52" x 66".*
Pat's view of a landscape through an arch was inspired by a photograph.

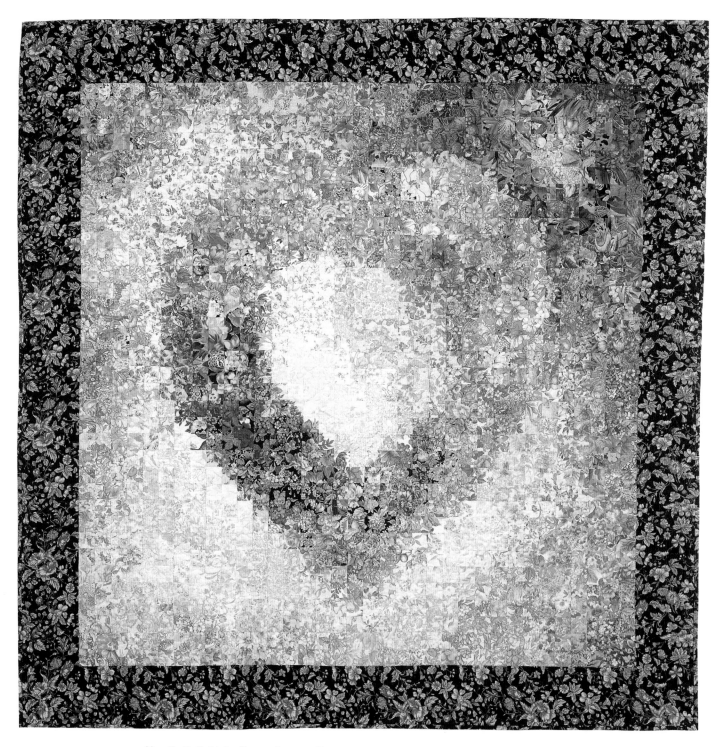

Heart's Delight *by Donna Ingram Slusser, 1993, Pullman, Washington, 64" x 64". Spring flowers contrast with the black touches to give a romantic, Victorian appearance. (Collection of Larry and Nicole Slusser)*

My Morning Garden *by Donna Ingram Slusser,*
1991, Pullman, Washington, 17" x 17".
Soft, hazy light filters through the center of the
garden in Donna's first watercolor quilt.

Ribbon Serenade *by Donna Ingram Slusser, 1993,*
Pullman, Washington, 60" x 60".
Color melts and scatters across the rhythmic
pattern of this composition, inspired by Susan
Kjelland's quilt, "The Road Less Traveled."
(Collection of Alan Martinson)

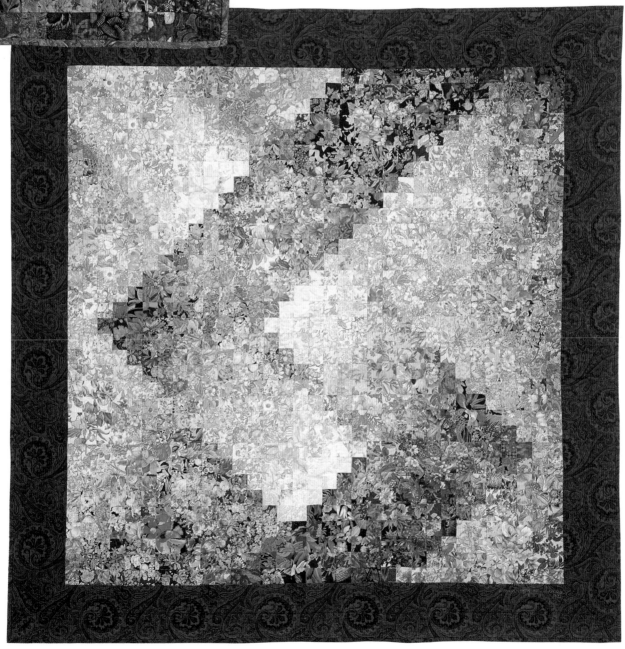

Tree of Heaven *by Lucy Neff Kittrick, 1992, Port Angeles, Washington, 30" x 37". The sunsets of Washington's Olympic Peninsula inspired these autumn colors. The quilt is dedicated to the memory of Lucy's friend and neighbor, Barbara Wiley.*

Through a Cottage Window *by Kerry Bloxham, 1992, Ferndale, Washington, 36" x 36". Sashing combined with a watercolor wash creates a look reminiscent of attic windows.*

My House Calls *by Sara Jane Perino, 1993, Pullman, Washington, 61" x 71".*
Janie's boys enjoyed helping her use unique and unusual fabrics, including a ghost and toys.

Urban Dawn *by Sharon H. Wiser, 1993, Pullman, Washington, 32" x 29".*
Inspired by a newspaper clipping, Sharon makes excellent use of pockets of color in this design.
The whimsical back of this quilt is shown on page 51.

Boston Sunrise *by J. J. Scheri, 1993, Eugene, Oregon, 35" x 27". The early morning city skyline in J. J.'s first watercolor quilt is reminiscent of her former hometown.*

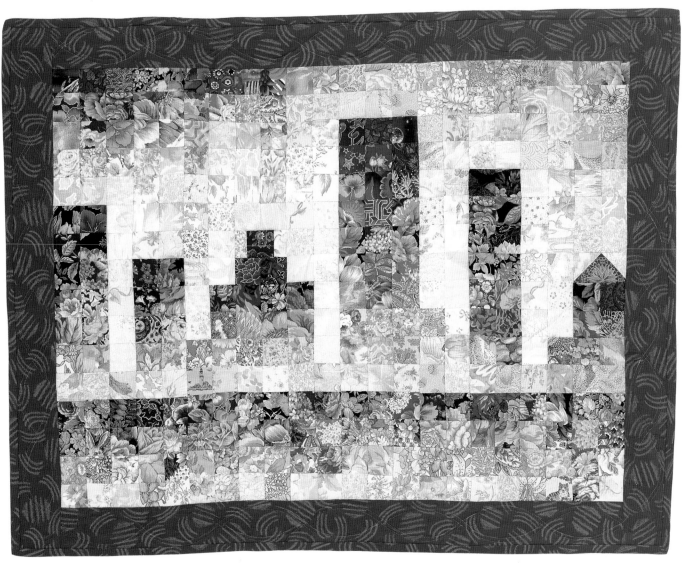

Universal Garden *by Barbara T. Wenders, 1991, Moscow, Idaho, 41" x 43".*
Inspired by the Garden Festival in Newcastle, England, Barbara made this quilt
while taking a Colourwash workshop from Deirdre Amsden.

Summer Afternoons *by Ellen Krieger, 1993, Pullman, Washington, 36" x 47". This design reflects impressions of a warm summer afternoon when the air feels heavy and is full of floating particles of color and light.*

Waiter, There's a Fly in My Maze *by Tammy Lydeen, 1992, Lewiston, Idaho, 32" x 32". A woven chain hangs diagonally. Look for the unique fly-print fabric hidden in this design.*

Liberty Star *by Kathleen H. Butts, 1992, Pullman, Washington, 18" x 18". Using variable stars and watercolor washes, Kathleen showcases her collection of Liberty of London™ fabrics in this quilt.*

Exit Four *by Karla Harris, 1993, Hope, Idaho, 38" x 38". The shaded rectangles in the center are rotated one-quarter turn to give a feeling of motion and light. Quilted by Wynona Harris King.*

Fade In, Fade Out *by Lisa Calhoun, 1992, Nezperce, Idaho, 38" x 38". Shaded watercolor bars with Ninepatch blocks express a meeting of traditional and contemporary effects.*

Floating Sphere II *by Daleah C. Thiessen, 1993, Pullman, Washington, 41" x 41".*
A watercolor sphere appears to float on a luminous background.

Blue Star Galaxy *by Anne Morton, 1993, Chewelah, Washington, 41" x 57½". Dark stars on a watercolor sky reveal the depth of space with all its color and movement.*

Galaxy *by Ree Nancarrow, 1992, Denali Park, Alaska, 37" x 37". This dramatic example of traditional blocks combined with watercolor techniques is highlighted by the half-star blocks in the border. Quilted by Wynona Harris King.*

It's Better Down Under *by Shirley Perryman, 1993, Pullman, Washington, 57" x 48". A visit to the Great Barrier Reef inspired this scene, which features appliquéd marine life.*

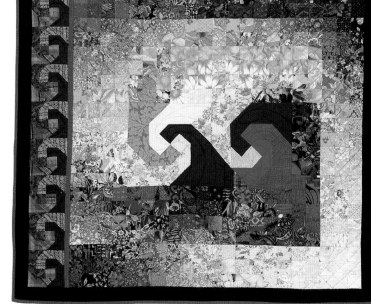

Iniki *by Ree Nancarrow, 1992, Denali Park, Alaska, 40" x 35". Two large Virginia Reel blocks spin into a wave that sweeps across the design.*

"Goraiko"—Rising Sun *by Yumiko Hirasawa, 1992, Yokohama, Japan, 58" x 58".*
This quilt uniquely exemplifies a meeting of East and West. The design was inspired by the
Japanese custom of watching the sunrise on New Year's Day and praying for health and
happiness, expressed beautifully here in the watercolor fabric medium.

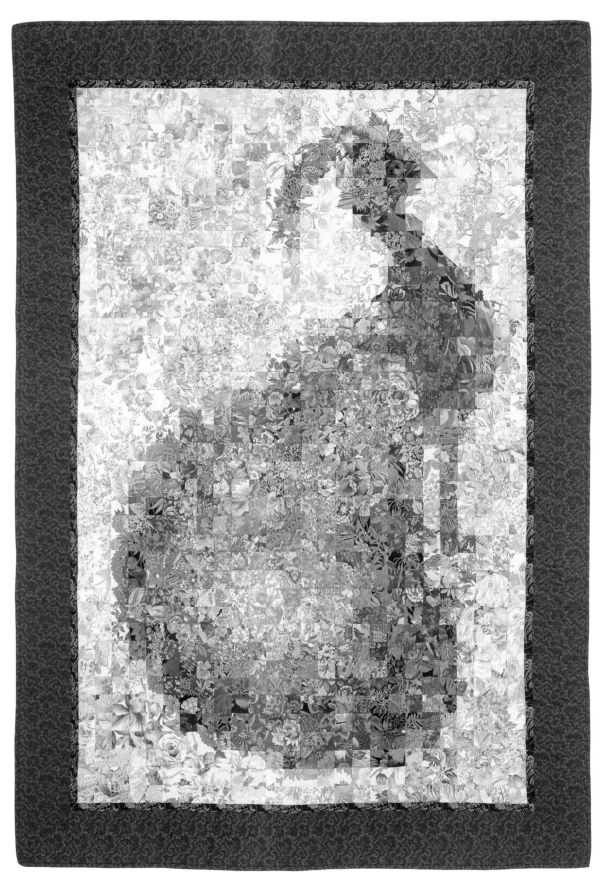

The Magnificent Toltec Bird *by Angie Adele Lewis Bingham, 1993, Hazelton, Idaho, 49" x 69". Based on an ancient Mexican tribal design, this bird is beautifully interpreted in watercolor fabrics.*

beyond Alces *by Karla Harris, Hope, Idaho, 1993, 32" x 41". Alaskan moose and wild flowers were the inspiration for this beautifully made quilt. Quilted by Wynona Harris King.*

Grizzly by Ree Nancarrow, 1992, Denali Park, Alaska, 25" x 21". An Alaskan bear is highlighted against a wild flower background surrounded by another frame of nature's beauty. Quilted by Wynona Harris King.

Window Box *by Patricia Maixner Magaret, 1992, Pullman, Washington, 27½" x 32". Pat re-created blossoms to produce a floral effect against a watercolor-graded wash. (Collection of Marilyn Bafus)*

Say It with Flowers *by Jeanie Renfro, 1993, Pullman, Washington, 34" x 38". Inspired by the Impressionists' floral paintings, Jeanie found this project a good excuse to shop for new fabrics to add to her collection.*

Blowing in the Wind *by Laurel Watson, 1992, Kingston, Washington, 46" x 43". Having all the pieces blow onto the floor during the design process gave new meaning to this title. An interesting border fabric gives this quilt a unique touch.*

Floral Fan *by Judy Mazzola Dobbelstein, 1992, Canfield, Ohio, 42" x 39". Clustering floral motifs gives an Oriental flavor to this innovative interpretation of a fan.*

An Artist's Palette by Rosy Ferner, 1992, Moscow , Idaho, 28" x 31".
The use of bright colors enlivens this rendition of the classic artist's tool.

Woven Ribbon *by Thine Lu Bloxham, 1992, Hayden Lake, Idaho, 22" x 27". Thine felt using all triangles was fun but more challenging than using squares.*

Pyramid Odyssey *by Judy Abdel-Monem, 1993, Moscow, Idaho, 56" x 35". Inspired by a picture in a travel brochure, Judy created depth and illusion in these washed shadings.*

Spring *by Lisa Nicholson, 1992, Eugene, Oregon, 23" x 23".
The center of this design contrasts nicely with the outside corners,
creating a light source within the quilt.*

Serendipity *by Myrtle
Fulfs, 1992, Pullman,
Washington, 22" x 22".
Light shining from one
corner "awakens" the other
color areas.*

Silver Lattice *by Margaret K.
Fortune, 1992, Richland,
Washington, 27" x 31". Watercolor
techniques produce highlights and
shadows that are accented by the
broderie perse flowers.*

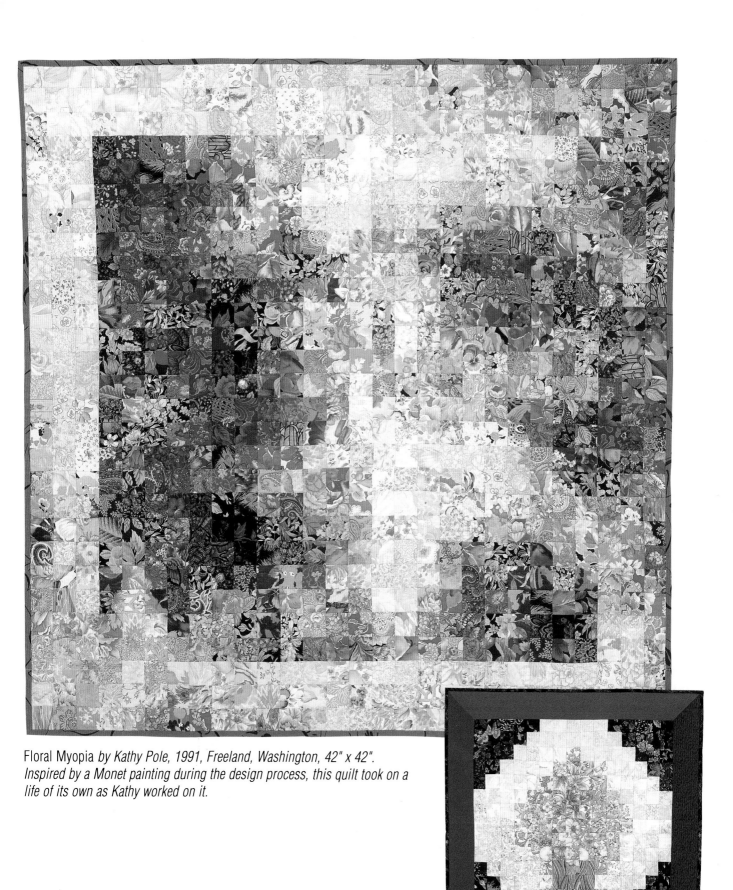

Floral Myopia *by Kathy Pole, 1991, Freeland, Washington, 42" x 42".*
Inspired by a Monet painting during the design process, this quilt took on a
life of its own as Kathy worked on it.

Garden Bouquet *by Annie E. Bacon, 1992, Pullman, Washington, 26" x 26".*
Combining floral lines creates a soft summer bouquet in a colorful fabric vase.

Religious Theme III: Everlasting Promises *by Donna Ingram Slusser, 1992, Pullman, Washington, 72" x 76". Glowing sunlight casts its reflection on a textured backdrop, highlighting the liturgical symbols of Easter and Pentecost.*

Stained Glass Garden *by Karen Pederson, © 1992, Seattle, Washington, 53" x 65".*
Octagons shaded from light to dark sparkle on a watercolor background.

Basic Quiltmaking Techniques

The following pages include basic quiltmaking methods for assembling and finishing your quilt.

ACCURATE SEAMING

To ensure that you are sewing accurate ¼"-wide seams, mark an accurate ¼"-wide sewing gauge on your sewing machine.

1. Cut along one of the grid lines on a sheet of accurate graph paper with four squares to the inch.

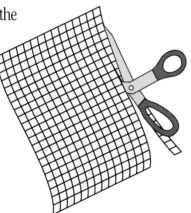

2. Slip the graph paper under the presser foot of your sewing machine, with the cut edge of the paper to the right. Lower the presser foot and needle so that the needle pierces the paper very slightly to the right of the first line on the grid. Place a piece of masking tape right next to the edge of the paper.

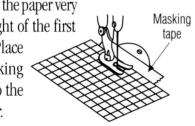

Masking tape

3. Make a ridge to guide the fabric edge by adding several layers of masking tape on top of the first piece, being careful to keep the edges aligned.

TIP

The distance from the needle to the tape will be a scant ¼" wide because you positioned the needle slightly to the right of the grid line. This is OK, especially when piecing a quilt top with as many seams as you have in a watercolor design. It makes up for the slight amount of fabric that is lost when you press a seam to one side instead of open as is done in traditional sewing.

CHAIN PIECING

Chain piecing—sewing pieces together without lifting the presser foot—saves time as well as thread.

1. Sew two squares together.
2. With the presser foot still down, sew several extra stitches beyond the edge of the squares. Do not remove the squares from the machine.
3. Insert another pair of squares under the presser foot and sew them together. Again, sew several stitches beyond the fabric, leaving the presser foot down.
4. Continue inserting new squares and "chaining." When you are ready to add a new piece to the first set of squares that were sewn together (the ones farthest away from the machine), clip the threads that join them to the other squares. Add the new piece, insert it under the presser foot, and continue the chaining process.

When chaining squares together to make a watercolor quilt, it is essential to use a pin to mark the top square of each row so the row does not get inverted while sewing. This marker will also help you remember that each new square is added to the end of the row that does not have a pin in it.

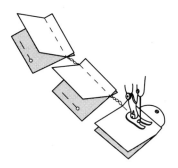

MAKING HALF-SQUARE TRIANGLE UNITS

Sometimes it is impossible to produce a diagonal line in a watercolor design where you want it without using a half-square triangle. When working at the design wall, find two squares that will accomplish the effect you want to achieve by using half of each one. Fold one of the squares in half diagonally and pin it on top of the other square. To sew the two squares together:

1. Place the squares right sides together and draw a line on the diagonal fold line, using a ruler for accuracy.

2. Sew on the line. Trim ¼" away from the seam, being careful to cut off the corners that will not be used.

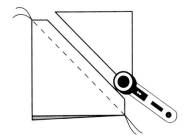

3. Press the seam allowance toward the darker half of the square. You now have a 2" square made of two half-square triangles.

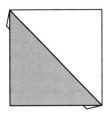

APPLIQUÉ

Curved appliqué designs applied to the surface of watercolor quilts provide a welcome visual break. If you plan to appliqué on top of your watercolor design, choose 100% cotton fabric for the appliqués. It is pliable and easy to manipulate. We also prefer two-ply cotton thread for hand sewing the appliqués in place. Match the thread color to the appliqué piece, not to the background.

Use needles called "sharps." They are longer than quilting needles and very slender. They are sized by number; the larger the number, the thinner the needle. Size 12 is the ultimate. The finer the needle, the finer your stitches will be. Use ½"-long sequin pins to hold the pieces in place on the background. Your sewing thread is less likely to get tangled around these short pins.

Preparing the Appliqués

1. Use a marking tool that leaves marks that you can easily remove. Trace the appliqué pattern onto the background fabric to mark the positioning lines for the appliqué pieces.

If the background fabric is light-colored, you can lay it directly over the pattern and see through it well enough to mark the lines. If the background fabric is dark, you may need to use a light box or take the project to a sunny window.

2. Number the pieces in the order they will be appliquéd. Start from the bottom layer, working up. If raw edges can be covered, make sure to appliqué these pieces first.

3. Make templates for each appliqué piece. Trace the shape directly from the pattern sheet. Do not add seam allowances to the templates.

4. Place the appliqué templates on the right side of the selected fabrics and trace around them.

5. Cut out each piece, adding approximately 3/16" allowance around the outer edges.

6. Place each appliqué piece on the background, following your positioning lines, and pin. Refer to the appliqué order as you place each piece.

Stitching the Pieces in Place

We prefer the needle-turn appliqué technique.

1. Start with a single strand of thread approximately 18" long. Tie a knot in one end.

2. Start stitching on a relatively straight edge and turn under the seam allowance as you stitch. Use the thumb and index finger of your non-sewing hand like a clamp, holding the turned seam allowance down on the background. Use the blind stitch to sew the edges of the appliqué to the background.

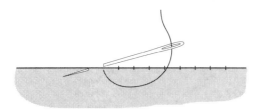

3. Clip the seam allowances at inside corners and on inside curves.

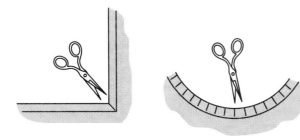

4. For sharp points and outside corners, stitch all the way to the tip of the point before turning under the seam allowance on the other side.

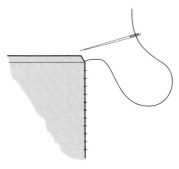

5. If an edge of one appliqué piece will be covered by another, it is not necessary to turn under the edge that will be covered. This avoids bulk.

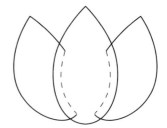

Appliqué side petals before central petal.

6. If a dark-colored background "shadows" or shows through the appliquéd pieces, cut it away from the back of the completed appliqué, leaving a 1/4" allowance of the background all around.

7. When the appliqué is completed, remove any markings that remain exposed on the surface of the quilt. Press the quilt top, right side down, on a towel to prevent "shine" and to maintain the relief.

Making Flower Stems

Bias Bars™ are handy tools for making narrow flower stems that curve gracefully across your quilt. These flat metal or nylon rods are available in varying widths; 1/8"- to 1/2"-wide bars are most commonly used.

1. Cut bias strips of fabric twice the desired finished width plus ½" for seam allowances. For example, if you want the finished stem to be ⅜" wide, cut the bias strip 1¼" wide.

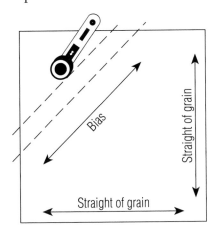

2. Fold the bias strip in half lengthwise with wrong sides together. Measuring from the fold, sew slightly wider than the finished stem width— just enough so you can slip the Bias Bar into the resulting tube.

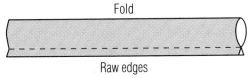

3. Trim the seam allowance to ¼" (narrower if your finished stem will be narrower). Slip the Bias Bar into the fabric tube and position the seam so it is in the center of the flat portion of the bar. Steam press the tube flat with the seam allowance to one side.

4. Carefully remove the Bias Bar. (It may be quite hot.) Position the stem on the background fabric and pin in place. Appliqué the edge of the inside curve first before you do outside curve.

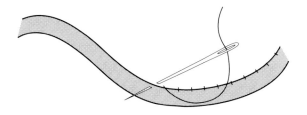

ADDING BORDERS

Most quilt tops require a border to contain the design and draw the eye into the quilt. For information on choosing border fabrics for watercolor quilts, see "Frame It!" on page 50.

You may attach borders with either straight-cut corners or mitered corners. Directions for both types of border applications follow.

Straight-Cut Corners

1. To prevent the edges of the quilt from rippling and ruffling, measure lengthwise through the center of the quilt top, not along the raw edges. Measure from top edge to bottom edge for the length to cut the side border strips.

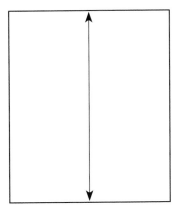

2. Cut two border strips of the desired width to match this length. Fold each border strip in half and place a pin at the center. Establish the center point of each half of the strip and mark with a pin so the border strip is divided into quarters. Repeat this marking process along the raw edge of the pieced quilt top.

3. Pin the border strip to the quilt top, matching the marking pins and easing to fit as necessary. Stitch, using a ¼"-wide seam allowance.

4. For the top and bottom borders, measure the quilt top across the center, including the side borders. Cut two border strips to this length and attach to the quilt top as described for the side borders in steps 2 and 3.

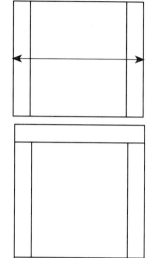

Mitered Corners

1. Estimate the outside dimensions (length and width) of the completed quilt with borders and add 3" to each measurement (for safety's sake). Cut border strips to these lengths. If you want to attach multiple borders to your quilt top, cut the required strips from each border fabric and sew them together for each side of the quilt. That way, you can attach them to each side of the quilt as one border.

2. Measure the quilt top through the center to determine the finished size of the quilt top and record the length minus ½" for seam allowances, and the width minus ½" for seam allowances.

Length - ½" = _____
Width - ½" = _____

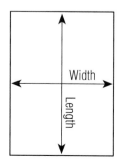

3. Find the center of each border strip and mark this point with a pin. Measure away from this point, in both directions, a distance that is half of the length measurement for the lengthwise borders and half of the width for the crosswise borders. Place pins at these points. Establish the center point of each half of the strip and mark with a pin so the border strip is divided into quarters. Place pins at these points.

4. Find the center of each side of the pieced quilt top and mark with a pin. Measure ¼" in from the outer edge of each corner and mark with a pin. When attaching the borders, this is the point where the stitching will stop or begin. Establish and pin the quarter marks on the quilt top as you did on the border strips.

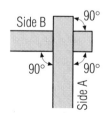

5. Pin the borders to the quilt top, matching pins and easing as necessary. Stitch, using a ¼"-wide seam allowance. Remember to start and end stitching ¼" in from each corner of the quilt top.

6. Miter one corner at a time. Spread a corner of the quilt smooth and straight on the pressing area, with the excess border strips extending from Side A to overlap excess border of Side B. Make sure that the two borders are at a 90° angle to each other.

7. Fold under the top excess border fabric of Side A at a 45° angle. Make sure the underneath border strips from both Side A and Side B line up exactly on the top and bottom edges. When you are sure that the corner is square and the resulting angle is 45°,

press the fold flat. This fold line is the sewing line for the mitered corner. Pin to secure.

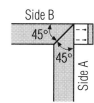

8. Flip the border of Side A up to match the raw edge of Side B so the quilt is folded on the diagonal, exposing the wrong side. Pin across the fold to secure. Stitch along the fold from the outside edge of the border toward the pieced center. Stop stitching when you are ¼" away from the innermost edge of the border. Trim excess border ¼" from stitching. Press well. Repeat with the remaining corners.

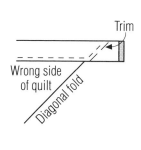

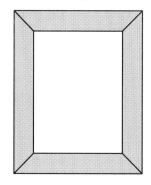

QUILTING

Quilting stitches hold the three quilt sandwich layers—top, batting and backing—together and prevent the batting from shifting. Before you can quilt, however, you must choose a design, prepare the backing, and choose a batting. After basting the layers together, you are ready to quilt by hand or machine.

Marking the Design

Review pages 52–54 for quilting design ideas for watercolor quilts. After selecting your quilting design, mark it on the quilt top before basting the layers together. Take care and use caution when selecting your marking tool. Always pretest any marking tool on sample fabrics used in your quilt to make sure the lines can be easily removed by washing. If you plan to machine quilt using straight lines, gentle curves, and/or free-motion designs, it may not be necessary to mark the quilting design on the quilt top.

Preparing the Backing

For best results, the backing should be the same fiber content as the front. We use 100% cotton and preshrink it. Make the backing at least 2" larger than the top on all sides. If it is necessary to piece the backing to make it wide enough or long enough, use three panels rather than two for a more pleasing appearance and to avoid a center seam. Trim off selvages and press the seam allowances open.

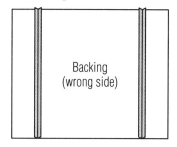

Review pages 51–52 for additional information on selecting fabrics for backings on watercolor quilts.

Selecting the Batting

Batting is the filler layer between the top and the backing of the quilt. Consider the fiber content and loft (height) of the batting when making your selection. Since most watercolor quilts become wall hangings rather than bed quilts, a low-loft or thin batting is most desirable.

Fiber content is a matter of personal choice. The 100% polyester batts are usually bonded to keep the fibers from shifting and they are very stable. Less quilting is needed to hold the quilt layers together. Polyester batting is easy to handle for both machine and hand quilting. However, the fibers of some polyester battings migrate to the surface of the quilt and create tiny "beards" or "pills."

Some of the older all-cotton battings required very closely spaced quilting to prevent the layers from shifting and separating during laundering. Some of the new 100% cotton battings are low loft and do not require such closely spaced quilting to hold the layers together. Cotton battings do not beard.

Cotton flannel also can be used as a batting. It must be prewashed and dried (several times if possible) since flannel tends to shrink more than the cotton fabrics in your quilt top. Because flannel is woven, you can space the quilting lines quite far apart. Quilts made with flannel batting are lightweight and have a flat look.

Cotton-polyester (80%/20%) battings are also low loft. The cotton content reduces the chances of bearding, and the polyester bonds the fibers together. That means the quilting lines can be spaced farther apart (every 2" to 3"). It is extremely important to follow the manufacturer's directions for presoaking or prewashing battings that contain cotton. They need to be preshrunk as much as possible before using them.

Polyester battings are easy for both hand and machine quilters to "needle." If you plan to machine quilt, pin baste the layers more closely as the polyester is more slippery than cotton.

Cotton battings are wonderful for the machine quilter to use because the fibers of the batting adhere to the top and backing fabrics. This helps prevent the shifting and stretching that causes distortion when you use a polyester batting. If you plan to hand quilt, experiment with stitching on a sample of the cotton batting. Some of them are difficult to "needle."

Pretreat batting if recommended by the manufacturer. Let all battings lie on a flat surface for a day or so before using to allow them to expand and take a big breath of fresh air after being stuffed into that tiny plastic bag. Cut the batting at least 2" larger than the quilt top on all sides.

Preparing the Quilt Sandwich

When the quilt batting has been selected and is "relaxed," the top and backing have been carefully pressed, and the quilting lines marked, it is time to put the layers together into a quilt "sandwich."

Basting the Layers Together for Hand Quilting

We recommend basting the quilt layers together if you plan to hand quilt.

1. Cut the backing and batting larger than the quilt top. Allow for a minimum of two extra inches on each side.
2. Lay the backing fabric, wrong side up, on a large, flat surface. Working from the center out, smooth out all wrinkles and either tape or pin the edges to the work surface, pulling the backing gently taut but not stretched.
3. Place the batting in the center of the backing and smooth it out from the center to eliminate any wrinkles.
4. Place the quilt top, right side up, in the center of the batting. Starting from the center, smooth it out so it is very flat and wrinkle free. Pin the edges to the batting and backing layers.
5. Working from the center out, pin baste the three layers together. Smooth any fullness toward the edges, adjusting pins at the outer edge if necessary.
6. Using a large needle threaded with white thread, baste the layers together diagonally, vertically, and horizontally. Space the basting rows 6" apart and remove the pins as you go. Lastly, baste around the outer edges of the quilt.

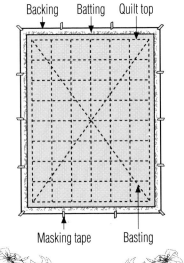

Backing　Batting　Quilt top

Masking tape　Basting

TIP

Pat also turns the excess backing fabric around to the front of the quilt and bastes it in place as a temporary binding. Her project looks tidy while she quilts, and her puppy can't pull at the batting.

Pin Basting the Layers
for Machine Quilting

Substitute pin basting for hand basting if you plan to machine quilt. Basting threads get caught in the foot of the machine while you are quilting. The layers also roll together and shift, causing stretching and distortion. In addition, it is difficult to remove basting threads when you have finished quilting because the quilting stitches have been made over them.

Take time to do a good job of pin basting. Layers that are well pinned are much easier to quilt. Careful pin basting helps prevent distortion and stretching during stitching and eliminates unwanted tucks and puckers on both sides of the quilt.

1. Fold the top of the quilt in half lengthwise and mark the center of the top and bottom edges with a pin. Mark the backing fabric and batting in the same manner. Measure the quilt top along the fold, from edge to edge, for the lengthwise measurement.

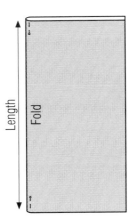

2. Working on a flat surface or table at least 3' x 5', mark the center of the tabletop on one of the short sides. Use a toothpick secured by masking tape to make the mark. This makes a center "bump" you can feel when centering the layers. Measure down the length of the surface from the marked center point until you reach the lengthwise measurement of the quilt top plus 3". Place another toothpick secured by masking tape on the table to mark this point. If the measurement is longer than the table, then mark the center of its edge.

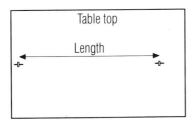

3. Fold the backing fabric in half lengthwise, wrong sides together. Place on the table, matching center marks of the backing with the toothpicks.

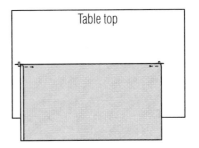

4. Unfold the backing with wrong side up, allowing the excess to hang over the edges of the table if necessary. Check to make sure the centers are still aligned by feeling the toothpick bumps. Carefully smooth the fabric open. Use binder clamps to gently stretch and securely hold the backing to one side of the table. Then attach more binder clamps to the opposite side of the table.

If your backing is long enough to reach the edges of the table, apply binder clamps to the remaining two sides. If not, apply several pieces of masking tape to the unclamped backing edges to secure it to the table. The backing fabric should now be taut but not stretched or distorted.

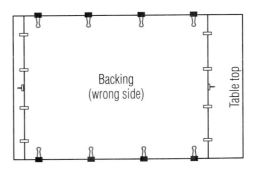

5. Fold the batting in half lengthwise and gently place it on top of the backing, making sure the center of the batting matches the toothpick bumps. Unfold it and carefully smooth it out so there are no bumps or wrinkles. Do not clamp to the table.

6. Fold the quilt top in half lengthwise, right sides together, and place it on top of the batting and backing. Match the center of the quilt top with the

toothpick bumps. Unfold it and carefully smooth the top. The quilt sandwich is ready for pin basting.

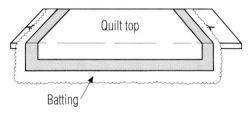

7. Pin the layers together, using #1, nickel-plated safety pins or extra-long straight pins. The safety pins take more time to clasp and unclasp but are very secure. Straight pins are not as secure but take less time to position (and they sometimes inflict pain while you are working!). Some quilters prefer to use a combination of pins, using the safety pins where extra security is needed and straight pins in the areas that will be quilted first.

Begin pinning in the center, working toward the outside edges, pinning every 2" to 3". Be careful not to scratch the surface of the table. If your quilt is larger than the table, remove the clamps and adjust the layers so a new section is on the tabletop, ready to pin. Reclamp the backing to the table on the unpinned side only. Continue until the entire surface is adequately pinned.

Hand Quilting

Many quilters enjoy methodically touching and savoring all those squares one last time by hand quilting. For hand quilting, it is advisable to use a thread with the same fiber content as the fabrics in your quilt. We recommend 100% cotton quilting thread.

Quilting needles are referred to as "betweens." The higher the size number, the finer and shorter the needle. Size 12 is the smallest. Most hand quilters strive to use a size 12 between because the shorter and finer the needle, the shorter and more closely spaced the stitches will be. Beginners may find it easier to start with a size 9 or 10 and then work up to the size 12. At first, concentrate on even stitches rather than the length. The ability to make short quilting stitches develops with practice.

Most quilters use a frame or hoop to support the quilt area in which they are working and to keep it smooth. A thimble is a must for the center finger of your quilting hand. Find one that is comfortable—not too snug and not too loose.

To hand quilt:

1. Thread the needle with a length of thread approximately 18" long and knot one end. Longer lengths tend to tangle.

2. Always start quilting in the center of the quilt and work your way out to the edges. Begin by inserting the needle through the top layer and batting only, about 1" away from where you want to begin your stitching line. Then bring the needle back out at the starting point. Give the thread a quick tug so the knot will pop into the batting—hidden forever.

3. Start with a small backstitch. Continue stitching, using a "rocking motion." Set the eye end of the needle in a groove of the thimble and guide the fabric in front of the needle with the thumb of the same hand. Place the index or middle finger of your other hand under the quilt. Make a small running stitch through all the layers.

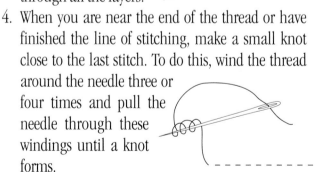

4. When you are near the end of the thread or have finished the line of stitching, make a small knot close to the last stitch. To do this, wind the thread around the needle three or four times and pull the needle through these windings until a knot forms.

5. Make one small backstitch and take a quick tug to bury the knot. Clip the thread tails at the surface of the quilt.

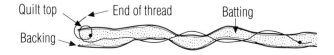

Machine Quilting

Your sewing machine must be in good working order for machine quilting. Good lighting is also very important. Position a table on the left side and one at the back of the machine to help support the weight of a medium to large quilt as you feed it through the sewing machine.

For the top of the quilt, use invisible, monofilament nylon thread to blend in with the many colors of the fabrics. Use clear, invisible thread in the light areas and smoke-colored invisible thread in the darker areas of your quilt top. These threads take on the colors of the variety of fabrics used in the watercolor quilt, leaving a depression along the quilting lines. They give the quilt the look of hand quilting as well as texture. Cotton thread stands out noticeably because it does not blend with the fabric colors. You can use variegated rayon thread instead of invisible thread if you prefer. In the bobbin, use a 100% cotton thread, size 50, 3 ply, in a color that matches the backing fabric. Wind several bobbins before you begin stitching to eliminate the frustration of stopping to wind bobbins after you start quilting.

 **TIP**

As you become more familiar and comfortable with machine quilting, you might want to try some of the metallic and rayon threads to highlight special areas in the water-color quilt. Try different brands to see which works best on your machine. Use them only on the top of the quilt; never put them in the bobbin.

When your machine is threaded correctly, check the stitches for balanced tension and make any necessary adjustments before beginning to quilt. A walking foot or even-feed foot is very helpful (essential, according to Donna) for tuck- and pucker-free straight-line machine quilting. It helps all the layers of the quilt "sandwich" to move evenly through the machine.

If you wish to make curves and free-motion quilting lines, set your machine for darning and attach the darning presser foot. Every machine is different so read your instruction book.

There are several methods of tying knots or securing the beginning and ending stitches. Donna uses a technique based on the fact that short stitches sewn closely together do not easily rip out. (Just try to take them out when you are doing regular sewing!) Set your machine for a short stitch length (.5 for European model machines or 20 stitches/inch for American models). Take 4 to 5 stitches at this setting when you begin a line of quilting stitches. Lengthen the stitch slightly (1.0 or 18 stitches/inch) and take 4 to 5 more stitches. Continue in this fashion until the setting is at 3.0 or 10 stitches per inch (or a stitch length that is pleasing to you) and then continue quilting. This method of securing the stitches should happen within the first and last inch of your line of stitching. (Reverse the process at the end of the line by gradually decreasing the stitch length until it is .5 or 20/inch.)

Machine quilting does not begin in the center and work toward the edges as in hand quilting. Instead, it is necessary to secure the layers and divide the top into manageable sections for further quilting.

To machine quilt:

1. Using the walking foot, stitch-in-the-ditch on the small squares as close to the inside of the border as possible.
2. Stitch through the center lines of the quilt, both vertically and horizontally. Sew additional vertical and horizontal lines as needed in order to make sections approximately 12" square.

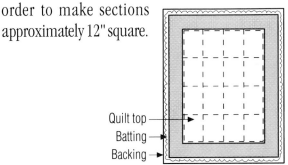

Quilt top
Batting
Backing

The stitched section lines secure the layers to eliminate shifting and distortion while you complete the remainder of the quilting. Occasionally, the quilt top will "creep" a little and there will be excess fabric as you sew. Apply more pins to the area in front of the foot in order to "ease" the fabric as it goes through the machine.

3. Now you are ready to quilt additional quilting design lines to enhance the beauty of your watercolor design. For straight lines or gentle curves, use the walking foot. As you quilt, be aware of the "section lines" and be careful when crossing them so that tucks and puckers do not form. Use extra pins as needed to ease in any extra fullness.

If your quilting design calls for more intricate, curved lines, set your sewing machine for darning. Read the instruction manual for your machine carefully. Use some of the free-motion techniques, such as stipple or "random quilting."

"Random quilting" is Donna's term for outlining flowers or other special motifs. The needle crosses over lines in a meandering style. When outlining flowers, leaves, and other shapes, sew ⅛" outside the lines of the flower or leaf rather than sewing directly on the lines. This technique adds relief to the design and enhances the shapes. When going from one area to another, loop and curve around to get there. Curved lines are more pleasing to the eye than straight lines, and they continue the "flow" of the watercolor design.

BINDING YOUR QUILT

When the quilting is completed, you are ready to bind the edges of your quilt. First, remove all basting, pins, and markings. Using a rotary cutter and ruler, trim away excess batting and backing. Make sure corners are square. Be sure the batting extends evenly to the outer edges of the quilt.

Double-Fold French Binding

A double-fold French binding cut on the straight or bias grain is a neat and very durable finish. If the quilt has curved or scalloped edges, you must cut the binding strips on the bias.

For double-fold binding, cut strips six times the desired finished binding width, plus ¼". The extra ¼" is for the fabric that will be lost in the turn of the folds. For example, if you want a finished binding ⅜" wide, cut the binding strips 2½" wide (⅜" X 6 = 2¼" + ¼" = 2½").

Calculate the amount of binding you will need to go around the finished quilt top and add an extra 20" for turning corners and for security and peace of mind. For example, if the quilt top measures 24" x 42", you will need 152" of binding (42" + 24" + 42" + 24" + 20" = 152").

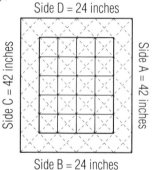

Side D = 24 inches
Side C = 42 inches
Side A = 42 inches
Side B = 24 inches

Straight-of-Grain Binding

1. After figuring the required amount of binding, cut strips from the crosswise grain of the fabric. One cut across the crosswise grain will give you approximately 40" of binding.

2. Sew the strips together at a 45° angle and press seams open.

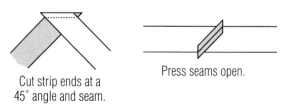

Cut strip ends at a 45° angle and seam.

Press seams open.

3. Fold the strip in half lengthwise, wrong sides together, and press.

Bias Binding

1. Cut bias binding from a square of fabric. To determine the size of the square needed, multiply the total amount of binding needed by the cut width of the bias strip you plan to use.

Total Binding Needed x Cut Bias Strip Width = X

Using a calculator, find the square root of X. The resulting number will be the size of the beginning square.

For example, for a 24" x 42" quilt requiring 152" of double-fold bias-cut binding that finishes to ½", you will cut bias strips 3¼" wide. (½" x 6 = 3" + ¼"= 3¼"). To determine the size of the beginning square, multiply 152" x 3¼" = 494. The square root of 494 is 22.2. Rounding this figure up to the nearest inch means you will need to start with a 23" fabric square.

2. Cut the required square of binding fabric and pin mark the center of the square at the top and bottom edges. Cut the square in half on the diagonal to yield two large half-square triangles.

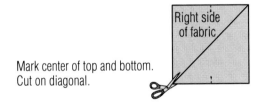

Mark center of top and bottom.
Cut on diagonal.

3. Place the right sides of the two triangles together so the pin-marked edges align. The ¼" tails will be exposed at each end, and the center pins will not match. Sew the pin-marked edges together with a ¼"-wide seam. Press the seam open.

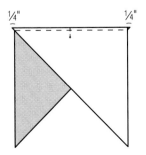

4. Measuring from bias side A, line up your ruler at the width required for the cut bias strips. Using your rotary cutter, make a cut approximately 3" long. Be sure the cut is parallel to side A.

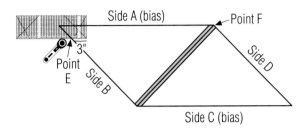

5. With right sides together, pull side B around to meet side D. Match point E to point F and pin raw edges together.

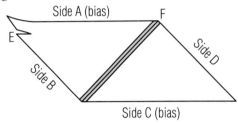

6. Stitch ¼" from the raw edges and press seam open. You will have a tube with a free-hanging, 3"-long tail at one end and an extension on the other end.

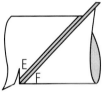

7. Place a rotary-cutting mat on your ironing board and slip the tube around the end of the ironing board, being careful not to stretch it. Cut a continuous bias strip from the tube as shown.

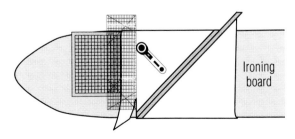

8. Fold the binding strip in half lengthwise, wrong sides together, and press.

Applying the Binding

1. Beginning near an inconspicuous corner of one side of the quilt, pin the binding to the front side of the quilt, with the raw edge of the end of the binding folded at a 45° angle.

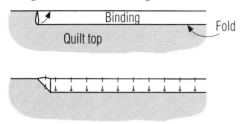

2. Use an even-feed foot, if available, to sew the binding to the quilt. Make the seam allowance the same width as the finished width of the binding. For example, if the finished width of the binding is ½", then you will stitch the binding to the quilt using a ½"-wide seam allowance. Be careful not to stretch the binding or the quilt top as you sew. When approaching a corner, stop stitching the width of a seam allowance from the corner. Backstitch. For example, if your finished binding is to be ½" wide, stop stitching ½" from the corner; backstitch and clip the threads.

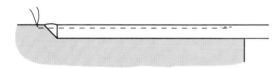

3. Turn the quilt. Fold the binding straight up and away from the quilt to form a 45°-angle fold.

4. Hold the fold down with your finger and bring the binding straight down along the edge of the quilt. There will be a fold in the binding that should align with the first side. Pin. Beginning at the top of the fold in the binding, stitch. This creates a mitered fold in the binding at the corner of the quilt.

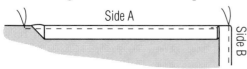

5. Continue sewing and mitering corners around the remaining edges of the quilt. When you reach the starting point, overlap the beginning of the binding ½" beyond the beginning stitches; backstitch and clip the threads.

6. Fold the binding over the raw edges to the back of the quilt and place the folded edge of the binding so that it hides the machine stitching line. Blindstitch in place, making sure stitches do not show on the front or back.

Back of quilt

7. At the corners, a perfect miter will form on the front of the quilt. Form a miter on the back by folding it in the opposite direction from the miter on the top side of the quilt; this distributes the bulk of the fabric evenly. Stitch the miters closed on both sides of the quilt.

ADDING A HANGING SLEEVE

Because of their artful nature, watercolor quilts are most often displayed on the wall and require a sleeve at the top of the backing for easy hanging. For the least noticeable sleeve, use a piece of the backing fabric or select one that goes well with the front and the backing.

1. To make a 4"-wide sleeve (finished size), cut a strip of fabric 8½" wide and as long as the top edge of the quilt. Turn under ½" at each short end of the strip and press. Turn under an additional ½", press, and stitch in place close to the fold.

2. Fold the strip in half lengthwise, right side out. Pin and stitch ¼" from the raw edge to make a long tube.

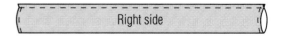

3. Center the seam on one side of the tube. Press the seam open and the tube flat.

4. Position the sleeve at the top edge on the back of the quilt just below the binding. Hand stitch all four sides of the sleeve to the back of the quilt, making sure the stitches do not go through to the front of the quilt. Be sure to leave the tube open at both ends.

5. Purchase a straight (not warped) piece of lath from a building-supply store. Cut it slightly shorter than the width of the top edge of the quilt and drill a hole near each end of the board. Position the lath on the wall where you wish to hang the quilt and mark the nail positions through the holes. Hammer nails into the wall and hang your masterpiece.

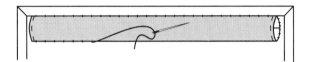

TIP

Since you will be making many watercolor quilts of varying sizes, write the name of the quilt on the board so you can easily identify it.

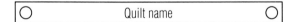

Quilt name

LABELING YOUR WORK

Quilt signatures and labels can be simple or elaborate. For historical documentation purposes, be sure to include:

- Your complete name (including your maiden name if you are married)
- Year that the quilt was completed
- Town and state where the quilt was completed

Any other information you wish to include is frosting on the cake, including:

The name of the quilt
Pattern name
Reason for quilt
Name of recipient
Occasion of gift
Hours of labor
Inspiration

The traditional place to sign your quilt is in the lower right-hand corner on the front, just like an artist. The best signature is one that is an integral part of the quilt itself. Use a permanent marking pen to leave a mark that cannot be removed. Other options include quilting the information into the quilt or embroidering it onto the front or back of the piece.

If you make a fancy signature label, use permanent ink to mark the pertinent information onto the quilt backing in the area that will be underneath the label. Make and attach the label, then quilt so the stitches go through all layers making it even more difficult to remove the information.

SOURCES

That Patchwork Place, Inc.
P.O. Box 118
Bothell, WA 98041-0118, USA
1-800-426-3126
Mail order for the Ruby Beholder™ tool.

The Calico Basket
412 Main St.
Edmonds, WA 98020
206-774-6446
Mail-order fabric swatch club.

The Cotton Club
P.O. Box 2263
Boise, ID 83701.
208-345-5567
Mail-order fabric swatch club.

International Fabric Collection
3445 West Lake Road
Erie, PA 16505
800-462-3891
Catalog and mail order with excellent variety of ethnic prints, Liberty of London™ prints. (A one-time $3.00 fee to receive catalogs.)

In The Beginning
8201 Lake City Way N.E.
Seattle, WA 98115
206-523-8862
Mail order for Liberty of London™ Tana™ Lawn prints and other watercolor fabrics; mail-order fabric swatch club.

Log Cabin Dry Goods
E. 3445 French Gulch Rd.
Coeur d'Alene, ID 83814
208-664-5908
Mail order for precut packets of watercolor fabrics and gridded vertical design wall.

The Patchworks
126 E. Main
Bozeman, MT 59715
406-587-2112
Catalog ($1.00) and mail-order fabric swatch club.

The Stitchin' Post
P.O. Box 280
Sisters, OR 97759
503-540-6061
Mail-order fabric swatch club.

There are other mail-order suppliers and fabric swatch clubs that advertise in current issues of quiltmaking magazines.

BIBLIOGRAPHY

Ash, Russell. *The Impressionists and Their Art*. New York: Crescent Books, 1980. A comprehensive history of the period and movement, including individual artists. 135 paintings reproduced in color.

Birren, Faber. *Color Perception in Art*. West Chester, Pa: Schiffer Publishing Ltd., 1986. An excellent source of information about color theory and special effects, written by one of the art world's foremost experts on color.

Bjõrk, Christina. *Linnea in Monet's Garden*. Stockholm, Sweden: Rabén & Sjögren Publishers, 1985. A delightful children's book about Claude Monet and an introduction to Impressionism for children of all ages.

Hargrave, Harriet. *Heirloom Machine Quilting*. Lafayette, Calif.: C & T Publishing, 1990. This book contains a wealth of information and is an excellent guide for those who want to explore machine-quilting techniques.

Kimball, Jeana. *Loving Stitches*. Bothell, Wash.: That Patchwork Place, Inc., 1992. Information on fine hand quilting is presented step by step in a clear, concise manner.

Kimball, Jeana. *Reflections of Baltimore*. Bothell, Wash.: That Patchwork Place, Inc., 1989. An extensive source on hand-appliqué techniques.

Petrie, Ferdinand. *The Big Book of Painting Nature in Watercolor*. New York: Watson-Guptill Publications, 1990. An excellent guide to painting nature. It also contains beautiful photographs that will inspire those watercolor artists who use fabrics as their medium.

Other books you will find helpful:

Gardens of the Impressionists Poster Book. Petaluma, Calif.: Pomegranate Calendars and Books, 1990. Featuring the work of many Impressionists, this book contains inspiration on every page.

Hopkins, Judy and Martin, Nancy J. *Rotary Riot*. Bothell, Wash.: That Patchwork Place, Inc., 1991. A good source for learning about rotary cutting and strip piecing.

Joyes, Claire. *Monet's Table*. New York: Simon and Schuster, 1990. Tempting treats to inspire the watercolor/Impressionist quiltmaker.

McClun, Diana and Nownes, Laura. *Quilts! Quilts!! Quilts!!!* San Francisco: The Quilt Digest Press, 1988. A comprehensive book for the beginning quiltmaker or for those who want to improve their techniques.

Murray, Elizabeth. *Monet's Passion*. Petaluma, Calif.: Pomegranate Artbooks, 1989. Photographs and sketches of Monet's garden inspirations and how he translated them into Impressionistic paintings.

Yenter, Sharon Evans. *In The Beginning*. Bothell, Wash.: That Patchwork Place, Inc., 1992. An inspirational book about one of the Pacific Northwest's best quilt shops, with patterns for some of their favorite quilts.

new and bestselling titles from

America's Best-Loved Craft & Hobby Books®

That Patchwork Place®

America's Best-Loved Quilt Books®

NEW RELEASES
1000 Great Quilt Blocks
Basically Brilliant Knits
Bright Quilts from Down Under
Christmas Delights
Creative Machine Stitching
Crochet for Tots
Crocheted Aran Sweaters
Cutting Corners
Everyday Embellishments
Folk Art Friends
Garden Party
Hocus Pocus!
Just Can't Cut It!
Quilter's Home: Winter, The
Sweet and Simple Baby Quilts
Time to Quilt
Today's Crochet
Traditional Quilts to Paper Piece

APPLIQUÉ
Appliquilt in the Cabin
Artful Album Quilts
Artful Appliqué
Blossoms in Winter
Color-Blend Appliqué
Sunbonnet Sue All through the Year

BABY QUILTS
Easy Paper-Pieced Baby Quilts
Even More Quilts for Baby
More Quilts for Baby
Play Quilts
Quilted Nursery, The
Quilts for Baby

HOLIDAY QUILTS & CRAFTS
Christmas Cats and Dogs
Creepy Crafty Halloween
Handcrafted Christmas, A
Make Room for Christmas Quilts
Welcome to the North Pole

HOME DECORATING
Decorated Kitchen, The
Decorated Porch, The
Dresden Fan
Gracing the Table
Make Room for Quilts
Quilts for Mantels and More
Sweet Dreams

LEARNING TO QUILT
101 Fabulous Rotary-Cut Quilts
Beyond the Blocks
Casual Quilter, The
Feathers That Fly
Joy of Quilting, The
Simple Joys of Quilting, The
Your First Quilt Book (or it should be!)

PAPER PIECING
40 Bright and Bold Paper-Pieced Blocks
50 Fabulous Paper-Pieced Stars
For the Birds
Quilter's Ark, A
Rich Traditions
Split-Diamond Dazzlers

ROTARY CUTTING
365 Quilt Blocks a Year Perpetual Calendar
Around the Block Again
Around the Block with Judy Hopkins
Fat Quarter Quilts
More Fat Quarter Quilts
Stack the Deck!
Triangle Tricks
Triangle-Free Quilts

SCRAP QUILTS
Nickel Quilts
Scrap Frenzy
Scrappy Duos
Spectacular Scraps
Strips and Strings
Successful Scrap Quilts

TOPICS IN QUILTMAKING
American Stenciled Quilts
Americana Quilts
Batik Beauties
Bed and Breakfast Quilts
Fabulous Quilts from Favorite Patterns
Frayed-Edge Fun
Patriotic Little Quilts
Reversible Quilts

CRAFTS
ABCs of Making Teddy Bears, The
Blissful Bath, The
Handcrafted Frames
Handcrafted Garden Accents
Handprint Quilts
Painted Chairs
Painted Whimsies

KNITTING & CROCHET
365 Knitting Stitches a Year Perpetual Calendar
Clever Knits
Crochet for Babies and Toddlers
Crocheted Sweaters
Knitted Sweaters for Every Season
Knitted Throws and More
Knitter's Book of Finishing Techniques, The
Knitter's Template, A
More Paintbox Knits
Paintbox Knits
Too Cute! Cotton Knits for Toddlers
Treasury of Rowan Knits, A
Ultimate Knitter's Guide, The

Our books are available at bookstores and your favorite craft, fabric, and yarn retailers. If you don't see the title you're looking for, visit us at **www.martingale-pub.com** or contact us at:

1-800-426-3126
International: 1-425-483-3313
Fax: 1-425-486-7596
Email: info@martingale-pub.com

For more information and a full list of our titles, visit our Web site.